Bea Alexandra Wintschnig

Sustainable Consumption and the Attitude-Behavior Gap

Drivers and Barriers

Bibliografische Information der Deutschen Nationalbibliothek:

Die Deutsche Nationalbibliothek verzeichnet diese Publikation in der Deutschen Nationalbibliografie; detaillierte bibliografische Daten sind im Internet über http://dnb.d-nb.de abrufbar.

Impressum:

Copyright © Studylab 2021

Ein Imprint der GRIN Publishing GmbH, München

Druck und Bindung: Books on Demand GmbH, Norderstedt, Germany

Coverbild: GRIN Publishing GmbH | Freepik.com | Flaticon.com | ei8htz

Table of Contents

List of figures IV

List of abbreviations V

1 Introduction 1

2 Conceptual foundation 3
    2.1 Defining sustainable consumption 3
    2.2 The attitude-behavior gap 5

3 Theoretical foundation 10
    3.1 Theory of Reasoned Action and Theory of Planned Behavior 10
    3.2 Norm Activation Theory 12
    3.3 Deficiencies of the TRA, the TPB and the NAM 13

4 Drivers and barriers of sustainable consumption 14
    4.1 Individual-related factors 15
    4.2 Environmental factors 29
    4.3 Conceptual model and additional remarks 38

5 Implications and future research 42

6 Conclusion 44

Bibliography 45

Appendix 68

List of figures

Fig. 1: Antecedents of behavior as originally conceptualized in the TPB 11

Fig. 2: Antecedents of behavior according to the NAM 12

Fig. 3: The main factors that have an impact on sustainable consumption 39

Fig. 4: More detailed representation of the drivers and barriers of sustainable consumption as well as factors influencing the attitude-behavior gap 41

List of abbreviations

NAM	Norm Activation Model
PBC	Perceived Behavioral Control
PCE	Perceived Consumer Effectiveness
SE	Self-efficacy
TIB	Theory of Interpersonal Behavior
TIB	Theory of Planned Behavior
TRA	Theory of Reasoned Action

1 Introduction

With adolescents around the globe demonstrating for a sustainable future and businesses increasingly embracing the idea of sustainable economic activities,[1] it is undeniable that sustainability has evolved from a niche topic into a mainstream one[2]. The consumption behavior of individuals plays a key role in enabling a sustainable future for the world.[3] This is manifested in the United Nations' 2030 Agenda for Sustainable Development with Goal Number 12 being "Responsible Consumption and Production".[4] In Germany, social justice as well as environment and climate protection rank in second and third place among the most important problems the country currently faces. However, only 19% of respondents think that enough is done for environmental and climate protection by German citizens.[5] This indicates a discrepancy between people's attitudes toward sustainable practices and the extent to which they actually act on them. This phenomenon is also frequently observed in the academic literature and is one of the few unambiguous insights concerning sustainable consumer behavior.[6] Generally, this topic has received increasing and considerable coverage in academic publications across various fields of research.[7] Nevertheless, there is a lack of understanding regarding the factors shaping sustainable consumer behavior, and researchers repeatedly comment on the need for clarity and further research.[8]

Therefore, this thesis aims to structure and discuss facilitators as well as obstacles of sustainable consumption identified in the literature to date and thereby give the reader an overview of the current state of scientific knowledge on this subject. This will be achieved through a systematic literature review. The thesis is structured as follows: Firstly, sustainable consumption, as well as the attitude-behavior gap, will be conceptualized, and reasons for the gap will be outlined. Subsequently, relevant theories for understanding consumer behavior in the context of sustainability will

---

[1] Cf. Bové et al. (2017), p.1; British Broadcasting Corporation (2019), p.1.
[2] Cf. Carrington, Neville, and Whitwell (2010), p.40; Mittelstaedt, Shultz, Kilbourne, and Peterson (2014), p.260.
[3] Cf. Sanne (2002), p.273; Tanner and Wölfing Kast (2003), p.883.
[4] Cf. United Nations (2019).
[5] Cf. Rubik et al. (2019), p.16f..
[6] Cf. Caruana, Carrington, and Chatzidakis (2016), p.215.
[7] Cf. Liu, Qu, Lei, and Jia (2017), p.427.
[8] see, for example Chatzidakis, Kastanakis, and Stathopoulou (2016), p.95; Abdulrazak and Quoquab (2018), p.16.

be discussed. This is followed by a synopsis of the drivers and barriers of sustainable consumption. Finally, implications for the effective promotion of sustainable consumerism will be derived, and future directions for research will be suggested.

2 Conceptual foundation

2.1 Defining sustainable consumption

The concept of sustainable consumption is traced to the action plan for sustainable development adopted in 1992 by the United Nations' Rio Earth Summit (Agenda 21).[9] Since no definition of the term was included therein, 'sustainable consumption' was first defined by the Oslo Symposium two years later. As this definition was not a scientific one, it was heavily criticized in the academic field.[10] Hence, several attempts were made to provide a more accurate and comprehensive characterization of the term, leading to a lack of clarity within the academic literature due to a myriad of available definitions.[11] A selection of these as well as related concepts can be found in the appendix (Appendix A). What becomes evident from these definitions is that conceptualizations of sustainable consumption should (a) capture the entire consumption cycle, (b) take into account ecological as well as social issues, (c) consider the well-being of the global population and (d) take a long-term perspective. With this in mind, the present thesis views sustainable consumption as the selection, acquisition, use and disposal of products and services that considers not only the consumer's own needs and wants, but also those of the current and future population in both an ecological and social respect.[12]

It is thus a very broad and multidimensional concept, which contains a range of different behaviors with varying levels of consumer commitment. It comprises, for instance, low-commitment acts such as buying fair-trade products but also actions that require deeper commitment like the reduction of the consumption level in general.[13] The practice of reduced consumption also represents the difference between the terms 'sustainable consumption' and 'consumption of sustainable products', as the latter merely refers to consuming products with positive social and/or environmental attributes[14], omitting the act of not consuming at all.

---

[9] Cf. United Nations (1992), p.18.
[10] Cf. Geiger, Fischer, and Schrader (2017), p.20.
[11] Cf. Peattie (2010), p.197.
[12] Cf. Vermeir and Verbeke (2006), p.170* (this is only the secondary source as the primary source is in Dutch); Di Giulio, Fischer, Schäfer, and Blättel-Mink (2014), p.54; Geiger et al. (2017), p.20.
[13] Cf. Prothero et al. (2011), p.32; Dermody, Hanmer-Lloyd, Koenig-Lewis, and Zhao (2015), p.1473; Scott and Weaver (2018), p.291.
[14] Cf. Luchs, Naylor, Irwin, and Raghunathan (2010), p.18.

Ethical consumption is often used as a synonym for sustainable consumption,[15] although it denotes consumption activities that are influenced by the consumer's ethical concerns.[16] It, therefore, differs from the aforementioned conceptualization of sustainable consumption, which does not necessarily have to be morally motivated. The purchase of environmentally friendly alternatives for reasons of superior taste or look can be classified as sustainable without being considered ethical.[17] Ethical consumption is commonly used to refer to problems with workers' rights, animal welfare or fair trade, but it includes environmental issues as well.[18]

Further similar and overlapping concepts can be found in the literature. These include 'green consumption' (inconsistent definitions exist in the literature, either referring to ecological issues only[19] or including social aspects too[20]), 'pro-environmental consumption or behavior' (concerned with effects on the natural and built world only[21]), as well as 'responsible consumption' (varying definitions throughout the literature with different widths of associated activities[22]). As this thesis views sustainable consumption as an encompassing and holistic construct, the just mentioned concepts all fall under this definition.

The cube model of sustainable consumption behavior by Geiger et al. (2017) is a framework that reflects the multifaceted nature of sustainable consumption. In addition to the already discussed aspects of (a) ecological as well as socio-economic impact and (b) different consumption phases, it highlights (c) the various areas of consumption in people's lives (e.g. food, housing, mobility) and (d) the impact of chosen behaviors (from low to high).[23] Although sustainable behavior comes down to its impact in the end, one cannot expect people to always be aware of the factual effect their consumption choices have. For the assessment of sustainability in consumption acts, the underlying pro-ecological or pro-social intention of the consumer therefore often counts. This is called an intent-orientated approach and it stands in contrast to the impact-orientated approach, which is concerned with the

---

[15] Cf. L. Johnstone and Lindh (2018), p.127.
[16] Cf. Cooper-Martin and Holbrook (1993), p.113; Kushwah, Dhir, and Sagar (2019), p.3.
[17] Cf. Strubel (2017), p.11.
[18] Cf. Shaw and Shiu (2002), p. 286.
[19] Cf. Tanner and Wölfing Kast (2003), p. 885.
[20] Cf. Moisander (2007), p.405.
[21] Cf. Kollmuss and Agyeman (2002), p.240.
[22] Cf. Valor and Carrero (2014), p.1110f.; Sudhanshu Gupta and Agrawal (2018), p.524.
[23] Cf. Geiger et al. (2017), p.20ff..

social and ecological consequences of the action at stake.[24] Both methods should ideally be combined for the promotion of sustainable consumption, meaning that in particular motives for consumer behaviors that have the highest sustainability impact should be identified and encouraged.[25]

2.2 The attitude-behavior gap

As previously mentioned, an issue that often arises during the exploration of sustainable consumption is a phenomenon that stems from social psychology and is called "attitude-behavior gap".[26] Several synonyms and very similar concepts exist in the literature, such as 'ethical purchasing gap'[27], 'ethical consumption paradox'[28], 'values-action gap'[29], 'words/deeds inconsistency'[30] or even '30:3 syndrome' (attributed to a study which found that 30% of people claim to be motivated to buy ethically featured products, but these only account for 3% of the market share[31]). The following section gives a more detailed outline in terms of definition and causes of this widely documented[32] matter.

2.2.1 Defining the attitude-behavior gap

Ajzen (1991) defines the attitude toward a behavior as "the degree to which a person has a favorable or unfavorable evaluation or appraisal of the behavior in question" (p. 188). In the simplest terms, it represents how a person feels or thinks about a certain behavior, for instance about buying groceries in zero waste shops. It should be clarified that 'attitude toward a behavior' refers to a *specific* attitude, which are to be distinguished from *general* ones, such as one's attitude toward waste avoidance at large.[33] The conceptualization of attitudes usually contains both cognitive (rational considerations like cost and benefit) and affective (experienced

---

[24] Cf. Fischer, Michelsen, Birgit, and Di Giulio (2012), p.73f..
[25] Cf. Geiger et al. (2017), p.19.
[26] Cf. Lapiere (1934), p.230ff..
[27] Cf. Nicholls and Lee (2006), p.369.
[28] Cf. Carrington, Zwick, and Neville (2016), p.21.
[29] Cf. Ertz, Karakas, and Sarigöllü (2016), p.3971.
[30] Cf. Newholm and Shaw (2007), p.257.
[31] Cf. Cowe and Williams (2000), p.5.
[32] Cf. Carrington et al. (2010), p.141.
[33] Cf. Ajzen and Fishbein (2005), p.173f..

feelings) elements.[34] The related concept of values, by contrast, is more basic. Values often underlie attitudes, which are linked more closely to specific objects or situations.[35] Beliefs are another concept related to attitudes. They refer to the information (the knowledge) a person has about an object, issue or person.[36]

An interesting and at this point noteworthy model is the one of dual attitudes by Wilson, Lindsey, and Schooler (2000). It proposes that people can hold two attitudes about the same object simultaneously, one implicit and the other explicit. While implicit attitudes are automatically activated and thus often not recognized, explicit ones are under conscious control as they require cognitive effort. The cognitive capacity to retrieve the explicit attitude determines whether or not the implicit attitude gets overridden.[37] This differentiation will be relevant for a later discussion.

For now, it is important to note that attitudes can be changed or altered relatively easy by new information or by both internal and external circumstances,[38] which already indicates that once-voiced attitudes are not always in accordance with future actions. This discrepancy is what the attitude-behavior gap is about. It refers to the inconsistency between a person's attitude and their actual behavior, and it has been identified by several authors in the context of sustainable consumption.[39]

In this context, it is important to distinguish between attitudes and intentions, the latter of which is defined as "instructions that people give to themselves to behave in certain ways" (Triandis, 1980, p. 203). They are conceptualized as people's motivations or decisions to perform a particular action. Representative responses have the form "I intend / plan to do behavior x" or "I will do behavior x".[40] Most models in the field of sustainable consumer behavior are based on the following core cognitive progression: Beliefs inform attitudes, these attitudes lead to intentions, and intentions, in turn, determine behavior. According to this framework, there may be a gap between attitude and intention as well as between intention

---

[34] Cf. Newhouse (1990), p.26; Ajzen (2011), p.1116.
[35] Cf. Homer and Kahle (1988), p.638.
[36] Cf. Petty and Cacioppo (1996), p.7.
[37] Cf. Wilson et al. (2000), p.104ff..
[38] Cf. Ajzen and Fishbein (2005), p.177; Schwarz (2007), p.642.
[39] E.g. Cf. Roberts (1996b), p.80; Boulstridge and Carrigan (2000), p.355; Carrigan and Attalla (2001), p364; Chatzidakis, Hibbert, and Smith (2007), p.89.
[40] Cf. Sheeran (2002), p.2.

and behavior that contribute to the overall discrepancy between what consumers express via attitudes and what they end up doing.[41]

2.2.2 Causes for the attitude-behavior gap

Four major grounds for the attitude-behavior gap can be determined from the literature. These are briefly specified hereinafter.

Deficiency of research methods

The first reason for the gap can be attributed to the applied study designs, which can result in several biases and other problems, such as inadequate data collection or errors made by informants in the prediction of their behavior. Apart from biases that are associated with decontextualization of the respondents and sample selection toward more sustainable consumers,[42] the most prominent bias is the social desirability bias, where respondents feel social pressure to provide socially acceptable answers.[43] Consequently, consumers tend to overstate their socially and ecologically responsible attitudes. This is especially true for self-reported survey instruments.[44] These are predominantly used in studies on sustainable consumption, with only a few researchers observing actual behavior.[45] It was found that when self-reported rather than actual behavior was assessed, lower attitude-behavior correlations were obtained.[46] A solution to this issue was recently suggested: Implicit attitudes should serve as an additional measure since they are more robust to external stimuli and therefore also immune to the social desirability bias.[47]

Another problem that can lead to discrepancies in the attitude-behavior relation is the unequal scope of measurement of attitudes and actions, as demonstrated by the following exemplary questions: "Do you care about the environment?" and "Do you recycle?", whereby the scope of the question referring to attitude is not as

---

[41] Cf. Carrington et al. (2010), p.142.
[42] Cf. Auger and Devinney (2007), p.363ff..
[43] Cf. Carrington et al. (2010), p.143.
[44] Cf. Chung and Monroe (2003), p.296ff..
[45] Cf. I. Davies, Lee, and Ahonkhai (2012), p. 38; see exceptions like Buttlar, Latz, and Walther (2017), p.155.
[46] Cf. Hines, Hungerford, and Tomera (1987), p.4.
[47] Cf. Govind, Singh, Garg, and D'Silva (2019), p. 1198.

specific as the one about the behavior.[48] Furthermore, as the measurement of attitudes and the execution of the discussed behavior are temporally separated, consumers tend to make mistakes in their predictions of future behavior (e.g. due to unavailability of the sustainable product at the time of actual purchase) or in their recollection of past behavior.[49]

Misleading monistic view of morality and personal goals

The second reasoning is not as well-explored in the literature as the social desirability bias, but it is, in a distant sense, also related to the just-mentioned insufficient capture of a person's attitudes. The core issues here are the multiple fragmented and competing identities of consumers.[50] Consumption choices are outcomes of balancing several potentially conflicting demands and desires. Thus, failure to engage in a sustainable consumption act does not necessarily mean that the consumer has incorrectly stated their attitude toward sustainable consumption. Instead, not all moral demands were considered, including the most decisive one that has overruled the attitude toward consuming sustainably. While a mother, for instance, may care for the environment, the duty of care for her child might outrank her environmentally conscious motivations.[51] The problem of duty conflicts is also reflected in the conceptualization of consumer choices as personal projects by Valor and Carrero (2014). According to this view, the gap is attributable to conflicts between different personal projects a consumer has, roles he or she plays and the influence of significant others.[52] This stresses the importance of holistically viewing all of a consumer's moral attitudes and the interactions between them.[53]

Rationalization strategies

Thirdly, rationalization strategies used by consumers to reduce feelings of remorse when past consumption choices contradict their attitudes may also contribute to the attitude-behavior gap.[54] Chatzidakis, Hibbert, and Smith (2007) revealed

---

[48] Cf. Newhouse (1990), p.28; Kollmuss and Agyeman (2002), p.242.
[49] Cf. Carrington, Neville, and Whitwell (2010), p.141.
[50] Cf. Szmigin, Carrigan, and McEachern (2009), p.229; Heath, O'Malley, Heath, and Story (2016), p.246.
[51] Cf. Heath et al. (2016), p.246.
[52] Cf. Valor and Carrero (2014), p.1119.
[53] Cf. Heath et al. (2016), p.246.
[54] Cf. Chatzidakis et al. (2007), p.89; McDonald, Oates, Thyne, Timmis, and Carlile (2015), p.1504f.; Gruber and Schlegelmilch (2014), p.39.

different before- or after-the-purchase justifications, labeled as "neutralization techniques" and describing mechanisms that consumers use to validate actions in violation of their attitudes. These encompass (a) denial of responsibility (e.g. lack of available information), (b) appeal to higher loyalties (e.g. financial constraints or inferiority of product), (c) denial of injury or of benefit (i.e. actions allegedly make little difference) and (d) condemning the condemners (referring to the unsustainable actions of others).[55] Additional authors extended these findings and discovered further justifications.[56] A table summarizing and explaining these can be found in the Appendix B. Justification strategies facilitate the gap by helping consumers minimize or even eliminate cognitive dissonance that usually arises from behaving against one's attitude. Neutralization techniques not only moderate the relationship between attitudes and behaviors but are also a determinant that can directly and negatively influence sustainable behaviors.[57]

The plethora of influencing factors

Lastly, a parallel and partly overlapping line of research took a modelling approach and identified potential variables that have a negative effect on behavior and therefore inhibit the translation of pro-environmental and pro-social attitude into actual actionsw.[58] These variables comprise both individual-related as well as circumstantial factors and change during different phases of the consumption cycle.[59] Since they not only explain the gap between attitude and behavior in particular but also represent obstructive factors of sustainable consumption more broadly, they are discussed as part of the overview of determinants in chapter four.

---

[55] Cf. Chatzidakis et al. (2007), p.89ff..
[56] Cf. D'Astous and Legendre (2009), p.264; Eckhardt, Belk, and Devinney (2010), p.430ff.; Gruber and Schlegelmilch (2014), p.40f.; McDonald et al. (2015), p.1512ff..
[57] Cf. Chatzidakis et al. (2007), p.95ff.
[58] Cf. Caruana et al. (2016), p.215.
[59] Cf. Mühlthaler and Rademacher (2017), p.191.

3 Theoretical foundation

To deeply understand sustainable consumer behavior, not only an awareness of reasons for the distance between attitudes and actions but also a knowledge of how behavior is generally formed is required. There are three classical socio-cognitive behavioral theories originally applied in other fields that have dominated the research agenda of sustainable consumption.[60] Their core statements are described and critically appraised below.

3.1 Theory of Reasoned Action and Theory of Planned Behavior

Fishbein and Ajzen's (1975) Theory of Reasoned Action (TRA) revolutionized the comprehension of the link between attitude and behavior by introducing the mediating role of intention.[61] It proposes that behavior is directly determined by an intention to perform the behavior and that this behavioral intention is, in turn, a function of subjective norms (the perceived social pressure of relevant others) and attitude toward the behavior.[62] In order to account for circumstantial limitations, i.e. when the individual lacks complete volitional control over the behavior, an otherwise identical theory was introduced under the name 'Theory of Planned Behavior' (TPB) which added a further antecedent of behavioral intention, namely Perceived Behavioral Control (PBC).[63] PBC represents the individual's "perceived ease or difficulty of performing the behavior" (Ajzen, 1991, p.188). It is deemed to reflect both the individual's anticipated impediments and past experiences. Not only does it indirectly influence behavior through its effect on intention, but it also has a direct influence on behavior in case it is a reliable predictor of objective behavioral control.[64] The three antecedents of behavioral intentions are underwritten by different kinds of salient beliefs held by consumers as demonstrated in the graphical representation of the TPB below:

---

[60] Cf. Chatzidakis et al. (2016), p.95.
[61] Cf. Hassan, Shiu, and Shaw (2016), p.220.
[62] Cf. Ajzen and Fishbein (1980), p.6.
[63] Cf. Ajzen (1991), p.182.
[64] Cf. Ajzen (1991), p.188; Bamberg and Möser (2007), p.16.

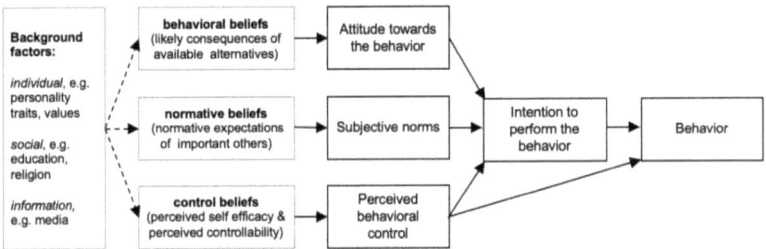

Fig. 1: Antecedents of behavior as originally conceptualized in the TPB[65]

As figure 1 illustrates, underlying behavioral, normative and control beliefs (further defined in the graphic) affect the antecedents of intention and can, in turn, vary as a function of a broad spectrum of different background factors.[66] In terms of control beliefs, it might be worth mentioning what perceived self-efficacy and controllability mean. Both are seen as lower-order constructs to PBC. While the former captures a person's belief about their capability to execute a desired action, controllability refers to the extent to which performing the behavior is up to the actor.[67]

Overall, behavior is viewed as a result of weighting costs and benefits (captured in the attitudes) as well as perceived social influence (social norms) and the difficulty of the action. Hence, the TPB regards individuals as utility-maximizing agents, acting rationally and consciously for their own good.[68] Many studies have tested whether the assumptions of TRA and TPB hold true. The results regarding the explanatory power vary significantly, from a mere R^2 of 0.0036 for recycling behavior[69] up to 0.84 for voting on a law that ensures a high reuse or recycling rate of bottles[70].[71] Possible reasons for this may be the variation in either the operationalization of the variables or in the types of behaviors the studies tried to explain. Consequently, the two theories were frequently criticized by researchers of sustainable consumer behavior. The presumably most prominent point of criticism is

---

[65] Own illustration based on Ajzen and Fishbein (2005), p.194ff.; Ajzen (1991), p.191ff..
[66] Cf. Ajzen and Fishbein (2005), p. 194.
[67] Cf. Ajzen (2002), p.672.
[68] Cf. Ajzen (1991), p.191ff.; Bamberg and Möser (2007), p.16.
[69] Cf. Davies et al. (2002), p.70.
[70] Cf. Gill, Crosby, and Taylor (1986), p.547.
[71] Cf. Hassan et al. (2016), p.224.

the lack of attention given to understanding normative, affective and habitual dimensions of people's behavior[72] and to contextual factors.[73]

3.2 Norm Activation Theory

As sustainable consumption means acting on behalf of collective beneficial outcomes in the long run, it is unlikely only a rational decision as suggested by the TPB.[74] Thus, pro-social motives might also play a role, which are covered by the Model of Norm Activation (NAM) by Schwartz (1977).[75] Norm activation describes a process in which individuals construct self-expectations with regard to pro-social behavior.[76] According to this less widespread theory, personal norms, conceptualized as "feelings of moral obligation, not as intentions" (Schwartz, 1977, p.227) are the only direct determinants of altruistic actions, such as sustainable consumption practices. Personal norms, in turn, are created by two personality trait activators, namely the awareness of the consequences of performing or not performing a behavior as well as the ascription of responsibility to oneself. De Groot and Steg (2009) provided strong empirical evidence that the NAM is a mediator model. According to this conceptualization, a person must be aware of the consequences of a behavior before feeling responsible for it,[77] as shown in figure 2 below:

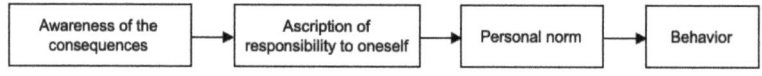

Fig. 2: Antecedents of behavior according to the NAM[78]

Studies show empirical support for the NAM,[79] and a meta-analysis revealed that integrating the NAM and TPB is useful, thereby suggesting that sustainable consumption behavior is probably best understood as a mixture of self-interest and pro-social motivations.[80]

---

[72] Cf. Shaw, Shiu, Hassan, Bekin, and Hogg (2007), p.33.
[73] Cf. Sutton (1998), p.1335; Carrington et al. (2010), p.148
[74] Cf. van Dam (2016), p.30.
[75] Cf. Bamberg and Möser (2007), p.15.
[76] Cf. Schwartz (1977), p.223.
[77] Cf. De Groot and Steg (2009), p. 443.
[78] Own illustration based on Schwartz (1977), p.223 and De Groot and Steg (2009), p.443.
[79] Cf. Harland, Staats, and Wilke (2007), p.328; Onwezen, Antonides, and Bartels (2013), p.149.
[80] Cf. Bamberg and Möser (2007), p.21.

3.3 Deficiencies of the TRA, the TPB and the NAM

The abovementioned theories have three shortcomings in common. For one thing, they do not explicitly or sufficiently take into account emotions. For another thing, they do not make allowance for unconscious or habitual actions (for a discussion of their influence see chapter 4.1.3).[81] Lastly, situational factors that intervene during the transition of intentions into actual behavior (see chapter 4.2) are not considered.[82] An attempt to overcome some of these insufficiencies has been made by Guagnano, Stern, and Dietz (1995) in their ABC model, which proposes behavior (B) is an interactive product of attitudinal variables (A) and contextual factors (C). It thus takes both and individual's self-factors and external components into account, such as institutional context and social influence,[83] but it still omits the influence of habits on behavior. Triandis' (1977) Theory of Interpersonal Behavior (TIB) is a model that does not suffer from this limitation. According to the TIB, intention – as in the TRA and TPB – is the immediate antecedent of behavior. Critically, habits also mediate behavior, and hence it allows for unconsciousness factors to guide behavior as well. Additionally, the TIB explicitly incorporates the purely emotional factor of "affect", which forms intention together with social factors and attitude.[84] Nevertheless, these two theories are rarely used in the literature on sustainable consumer behavior, which is why they are not discussed in detail here.

What becomes certain from the discussion above, however, is that understanding the behavior of individuals in the field of sustainability is a complex and multifaceted issue, which is influenced by a wide variety of factors. This can be ascribed to the functional and hedonic nature of sustainability and the nuanced and emotional experiences of individuals when dealing with it.[85]

---

[81] Cf. Ajzen and Fishbein (2000), p.3ff.; J. Davies et al. (2002), p.98.; Conner, Godin, Sheeran, and Germain (2013), p.264.

[82] Cf. Carrington et al. (2010), p.142.

[83] Cf. Guagnano et al. (1995), p.701ff..

[84] Cf. Triandis (1977), page is missing as the source could not be found. Information is therefore assembled from different articles citing Triandis (1977), e.g. Ozaki (2011), p.3.

[85] Cf. Dolan (2002), p.174f.; Schaefer and Crane (2005), p.85.

4 Drivers and barriers of sustainable consumption

The following compilation of the academic literature dealing with barriers and drivers of sustainable consumer acts is intended to bring more clarity into this complex topic. The review of the status quo of research was carried out as follows: Synonyms for 'sustainable consumption' and 'attitude-behavior gap' were determined and entered in the search engine of the databases of EBSCOhost and ScienceDirect. Filters concerning the article type and language helped to narrow down the results, whose abstracts were subsequently screened to identify papers that explored individual leisure behavior and discovered drivers or barriers thereof. An additional selection criterion applied was the quality of the article, measured by the ranking of the journal where it was published. While reading the filtered articles, a literature table was created and the bibliographies were screened for additional useful articles. In the end, the results of 118 papers have been incorporated into the overview of determining factors below. The purchasing phase of the consumption cycle lies in the focus of these articles, with buying groceries being a particularly dominant theme.[86] The post-purchase behavior recycling has also received considerable coverage in the literature, with less attention given to behaviors like reduced consumption and its various practices such as repurposing, which describes using a product for something for which it was not initially intended.[87] Further statistics on the key characteristics of the reviewed literature can be found in the appendix (Appendices C, D and E).

The determinants found in the literature review were broadly subdivided into individual-related factors and environmental factors. Within each of these two categories, related determining factors were grouped. No differentiation was made between drivers and barriers in the listing because in the majority of cases, one factor represents both a facilitator and an obstacle, depending on the nature of the manifestation or whether the factor is absent or present (e.g. a consumer's control orientation is a facilitator if he or she has an internal locus of control, whereas it is an inhibitor in case of an external one). Following the written description below, a graphical illustration of the determinants is presented.

---

[86] Cf. Cf. Chatzidakis et al. (2016), p.96.
[87] Cf. Tilikidou and Delistavrou (2008), p.61; Scott and Weaver (2018), p. 291.

4.1 Individual-related factors

This category comprises variables that positively or negatively affect consumers' decision-making and behavior from within. They are strongly dependent on the individual but may not be completely detached from external influences.

4.1.1 Socio-demographics

Studies exploring the socio-demographic characteristics of sustainable consumers examined variables like age, income level, educational level, gender, and religiosity, and they provided mixed results.[88] A meta-analysis on responsible environmental behavior found the following correlations between variable and behavior which reflect results of later studies as well: (a) educational level: 0.185, (b) income: 0.162, (c) age: -0.151 and (d) gender: 0.075. For the last two variables, the standard deviation was larger than the correlation itself, indicating a tenuous relationship.[89] Due to the generally inconsistent and thus inconclusive results demographic variables provide, they are said to be of very limited help in understanding the adoption of sustainable practices.[90] Moreover, differences in gender, for instance, were attributed to the underlying personality traits which are typically observed in women vs. men.[91] Consequently, research focused on understanding intrapersonal factors,[92] and the same approach is taken in this thesis. Socio-demographical factors further cannot be changed by promotion measures, which is another reason why they are not elaborated at this point.

4.1.2 Personal characteristics and value orientation

This cluster discusses the character traits and the personal value orientation of consumers, which are two closely interrelated factors and are mostly developed in the early years or are even innate. They do not specifically relate to sustainability but represent the general basic disposition of a person. It follows from this that such determinants are not easily changed by either the individuals themselves or

---

[88] Cf. Davies (2002), p.84; Rowlands, Scott, and Parker (2003), p.44; De Pelsmacker, Janssens, Sterckx, and Mielants (2005), p.522; Grønhøj and Ölander (2007), p.218; Tilikidou and Delistavrou (2008), p.66; Doran (2009), p.559f.; Bateman and Valentine (2010), p.393; Graafland (2017), p.121; Park and Lin (2018), p.5.
[89] Cf. Hines et al. (1987), p.5f..
[90] Cf. Diamantopoulos, Schlegelmilch, Sinkovics, and Bohlen (2003), p.477
[91] Cf. Brough, Wilkie, Jingjing, Isaac, and Gal (2016), p.568
[92] Cf. Buerke, Straatmann, Lin-Hi, and Müller (2016), p.965

external influences like marketing efforts. However, they are still viewed as important antecedents of a person's decision to act in a sustainable manner[93] and in some cases also as a driver of the translation of attitudes regarding sustainability into behavior, which is why they are discussed below.

Regarding influencing personal characteristics, the following were identified as relevant by researchers:

- Altruism, i.e. active concern for the welfare of others, has a significant positive influence on sustainable consumer behavior.[94] Moreover, altruistic personal values were found to contribute to feelings of guilt after a consumer has opted for the non-sustainable choice,[95] thereby they might indirectly drive sustainable consumption (see section 4.1.3).
- Commitment to one's beliefs in general also increases the likelihood that the consumer follows through on their beliefs regarding sustainability.[96]
- Emotional intelligence also facilitates consuming sustainably as it moderates the effect of environmental engagement on behavior.[97]
- An individual's locus of control, the perception of whether one has the ability to bring about change through their behavior instead of attributing change to chance or powerful others (such as the government) is seen as a driver when the individual has an internal locus of control and viewed as a barrier in case of an external locus of control.[98]
- Long-term orientation was found to positively influence attitudes toward sustainable acts.[99] This might be explained by the fact that sustainability issues involve a long-time horizon, which is, in turn, generally viewed as an inhibitor to the adoption of sustainable practices.[100]

---

[93] Cf. E.g. Barbarossa and Pelsmacker (2016), p.229
[94] Cf. Straughan (1999), p.568; Rowlands et al. (2003), p.45; Pepper, Jackson, and Uzzell (2009), p.133; Song and Kim (2018), p.1162ff..
[95] Cf. Antonetti and Maklan (2014b) p.723.
[96] Cf. Maxwell-Smith, Conway, Wright, and Olson (2018), p.851.
[97] Cf. Kadic-Maglajlic, Arslanagic-Kalajdzic, Micevski, Dlacic, and Zabkar (2019), p.8.
[98] Cf. Hines et al. (1987), p.5; McCarty and Shrum (2001), p.101; Tilikidou and Delistavrou (2008), p.69; Yang and Weber (2019), p.63.
[99] Cf. Leonidou, Leonidou, and Kvasova (2010), p.1337.
[100] Cf. Zaval, Markowitz, and Weber (2015), p.235.

- A person's openness and affinity for new ideas proved to be an essential factor in understanding how attitudes are causally related to sustainable consumer behavior.[101]
- Self-discipline is a trait demonstrated by sustainable consumers in qualitative studies, as it allows them, for instance, to resist the temptation to buy cheap but unsustainable products.[102]

Besides personality traits, the related value orientations and their influence on sustainable consumer behavior have been examined by several researchers and proved to be positively or negatively related to behavior.[103] One of the concordant results of these studies is that egoistic values, also called self-enhancement or power values, show an inverse relationship to pro-environmental and pro-social attitudes and behaviors. This is because they trigger actions that only take into account oneself and not the others,[104] which stands in contrast with the positive influencing trait altruism. Universalism values also emphasize prosocial concern and are proven to have a favorable influence on sustainable consumer behavior.[105] Interestingly, a study revealed that the predominance of universalism values as opposed to benevolence values, which, however, are similar to universalism values since they are both focused on supporting others, distinguish loyal fair trade consumers from those who buy fair trade only intermittently. This is because universalism values concern *all* people, whereas benevolence values focus on a person's own group, the so-called in-group.[106] It was concluded that an overriding sense of responsibility to one's in-group prevents some consumers from buying pro-social products as this includes sharing resources with members of one's out-group, for example farmers in remote regions of the world.[107] Other findings in the field of values state that consumers who hold traditional values (e.g. being humble or not having extreme ideas or feelings) have a higher tendency to buy sustainable

---

[101] Cf. Grob (1995), p.215; Englis and Phillips (2013), p. 169; Song and Kim (2018), p.1169.
[102] Cf. Shaw, Grehan, Shiu, Hassan, and Thomson (2005), p.194; Johnstone and Tan (2015), p. 316.
[103] See, for instance, Stern and Dietz (1994), p.65ff.; Poortinga, Steg, and Vlek (2004), p.87f..
[104] Cf. Urien and Kilbourne (2011), p.71.
[105] Cf. Thøgersen and Olander (2002), p.623; Shaw et al. (2005), p.196; Doran (2009), p.559; Thøgersen and Zhou (2012), p.327; Eberhart and Naderer (2017), p.1165.
[106] Cf. Doran (2009), p.559.
[107] Cf. Doran (2010), p.536.

products than power seekers.[108] Environmentally responsible consumption is also more likely to be shown by consumers holding generativity values (the belief that one's current behavior has consequences for future generations).[109] Furthermore, while materialism is viewed as negatively impacting sustainable consumption in Western countries, the influence for Chinese people is positive, indicating different meanings of materialism between countries and thus cultural differences in sustainable consumer behavior.[110] Other cultural values such as collectivism, which is predominant in Asian countries, showed positive relations to responsible consumption.[111] This is because individuals valuing collectivism are more likely to subordinate their own interests in pursuit of group interests, which might be necessary for sustainable consumer acts.[112] This finding supports the notion that there are differences in sustainable consumer behavior between individuals of disparate cultures.

Related to values is the more concrete concept of personal norms or moral obligations, defined above. Even though it was found by one study that personal norms play no significant role in predicting green food purchases,[113] it is generally seen as an important driver for sustainable behavior,[114] as demonstrated by its key role in the NAM as well.[115] In some cases, consumers even integrate environmental motives into their self-identity, thereby enhancing sustainable consumption behavior[116] since this integration mediates the relationship between values and behavior.[117] However, the aspiration to maintain a positive self-perception can result in the negative effect of self-defensive behaviors such as denigrating others who act more sustainably.[118]

---

[108] Cf. Vermeir and Verbeke (2008), p.549.
[109] Cf. Urien and Kilbourne (2011), p.69f..
[110] Cf. Dermody et al. (2015), p. 1487.
[111] Cf. Chan (2001), p.404; Leonidou et al. (2010), p.1335.
[112] Cf. Chan (2001), p.392.
[113] Cf. Tanner and Wölfing Kast (2003), p.891.
[114] Cf. Hunecke, Blöbaum, Matthies, and Hoeger (2001), p.844; Davies (2002), p.93; Harland et al. (2007), p.332; Barbarossa and Pelsmacker (2016), p.243.
[115] Cf. Schwartz (1977), p.223.
[116] Cf. Barbarossa and Pelsmacker (2016), p.238; Carfora et al. (2019), p.7.
[117] Cf. Dermody et al. (2015), p.1489.
[118] Cf. Zane, Irwin, and Walker Reczek (2015), p.346f..

In order to complete the discussion on values, it can be stated that the so-called "consumerism paradigm", which has established in most cultures and thus peoples' values, is another factor that is holding people back from consuming in a sustainable manner. This is due to the paradigm's underlying assumptions that more consumption makes happier, that perpetual growth is what people should strive for and that humans have the right to exploit natural resources.[119] Since consumption is mainly a cultural process and results from norms rather than needs, scientists concluded that a cultural shift to a low consumption paradigm is necessary.[120] This also indicates that individuals are influenced by others in their behavior, as elaborated in section 4.2.3.

4.1.3 Non-cognitive factors

The next cluster has something in common with the preceding one, which is that associated factors cannot easily be changed by marketing measures. Non-cognitive factors are characterized by the fact that consumers are not consciously aware of them and thus are not fully in control of the effects they bring about. Although their contribution is, as aforementioned, underrepresented in the TRA, TPB and NAM,[121] they are of great relevance to actual sustainable consumer behavior, as shown hereinafter.

Emotions

Generally, both positive and negative emotions can not only be an outcome of but also a generator or inhibitor of sustainable behavior.[122] To begin with, it was found that emotional affinity or proximity toward nature enhances the tendency to act pro-environmentally.[123] This feeling is strengthened by past and present experiences in natural environments.[124] From this it can be inferred that the increasing urbanization and the related decrease of time spent in nature may aggravate sustainable behaviors in the future.[125]

---

[119] Cf. Assadourian (2010), p. 189.
[120] Cf. Dolan (2002), p.172ff.; Lorenzoni, Nicholson-Cole, and Whitmarsh (2007), p.456.
[121] Cf. Russell, Young, Unsworth, and Robinson (2017), p.108.
[122] Cf. Gregory-Smith, Smith, and Winklhofer (2013), p.1203.
[123] Cf. Kals, Schumacher, and Montada (1999), p.197; Chan (2001), p.403; Kunchamboo, Lee, and Brace-Govan (2017), p.131.
[124] Cf. Kals et al. (1999), p.193.
[125] Assumption also based on M. L. Johnstone and Tan (2015), p.317

More general negative emotions, such as anger or guilt, are associated with greater intentions to engage in sustainable consumption. However, this intention does not translate into behavior, as results of a survey studying food waste behavior revealed. Participants who experienced more negative emotion when thinking about food waste ended up wasting more food although they intended differently.[126] The same is true for positive anticipated emotions like pride or excitement. A study in the field of saving electricity found that positive anticipated emotions boosted intentions, which did not result in actual saving behavior. It was suggested that this could be grounded in the fact that individuals may think that they can save electricity in the future, which makes not saving in the present forgivable.[127] A second possible explanation is that individuals may want to avoid having to think about the negative situation (like wasting food) and therefore make no effort to change it.[128]

The first explanation already indicates that emotions may play a role in the application of the aforementioned rationalization techniques which are used by consumers after having engaged in a behavior that is not in line with their attitude.[129] Antonetti and Maklan (2014) show that feelings of guilt and pride have an impact on the use of neutralization techniques and the consumer's perceptions of agency and thereby regulate sustainable consumption. More specifically, experiencing guilt and pride forces consumers to recognize the causal link between their own actions and certain sustainability outcomes. As a consequence, their ability to neutralize their sense of personal responsibility decreases, leading to an increased sense of effectiveness in turn and thus to a positive relationship between guilt/pride and intentions to engage in sustainable consumer behavior.[130] Nevertheless, Gregory-Smith et al. (2013) argued that the cognitive dissonance that is usually accompanied by emotions of guilt and regret is relieved by specific strategies (e.g. promising oneself to act differently next time), thereby reducing or even ruining the suggested positive effect of such emotions on future behavior. They additionally found, however, that the experience of positive post-decision emotions

---

[126] Cf. Russell et al. (2017), p.111.
[127] Cf. Wang, Lin, and Li (2018), p.177.
[128] Cf. Russell et al. (2017), p.12.
[129] Cf. Chatzidakis et al. (2007), p.97; Bray, Johns, and Kilburn (2011), p.603.
[130] Cf. Antonetti and Maklan (2014b), p.129.

like pride or happiness, which arise when the consumer made a choice in line with their beliefs, will reinforce such sustainable decisions in the future.[131]

Furthermore, the meta-analysis of Bamberg and Möser (2007) revealed that feelings of guilt are a significant predictor of the personal moral norm, the immediate determinant of behavior in the NAM.[132] Others found that anticipated emotions form the underlying mechanism through which personal norms guide behavior. They motivate individuals to behave in accordance with their moral standards in order to not only avoid negative emotions, but also to aim for positive ones.[133] This contradicts the finding mentioned above that did not find this enhancing effect of positive anticipated emotions on behavior.[134] The reason why guilt and pride are regarded by some as motivational is because they initiate a process of self-evaluation, i.e. a comparison between the actions of the actual self and those of the 'ideal' self or of the self that others want to see.[135]

Lastly, guilt influences the perception of the ease of performing an action as well as its outcomes. If an individual anticipates stronger feelings of guilt when not acting in a sustainable manner, they tend to view engaging in the sustainable alternative as easier and associate more positive personal consequences with opting for this option.[136]

Habits

The second non-cognitive determinant are habits, which were, to recall, just like emotions proposed to affect behavior in the TIB.[137] They may also be viewed as influences on a person's controllability and thus their PBC, an important determinant of behavior in the TPB.[138] Habits are defined as "relatively stable behavioral patterns" (Verplanken, Aarts, Knippenberg, & Knippenberg, 1994, p. 287) that are executed without deliberate considerations, which means that an automatic response guides them.[139] This requires less cognitive effort than what would be

---

[131] Cf. Gregory-Smith et al. (2013), p.1214f.
[132] Cf. Bamberg and Möser (2007), p. 21.
[133] Cf. Onwezen et al. (2013), 150f..
[134] Cf. Wang et al. (2018), p.177.
[135] Cf. Gregory-Smith et al. (2013), p.1203.
[136] Cf. Bamberg and Möser (2007), p.21.
[137] Cf. Triandis (1977), page is missing for the reason explained above.
[138] Cf. Carrington et al. (2010), p.146.
[139] Cf. Verplanken et al. (1994), p.287.

required for conscious reasoning.[140] Hence, habitual behavior may involve selective attention, leading consumers to concentrate on information that confirms their choices and disregard what is not in line with their habits.[141] Since habits tend to be mechanically prompted by contextual and environmental factors, they hinder consumers to switch to an alternative behavior,[142] simply put because they forget that they intended to act differently.[143] Habits were found to play a greater role for low-involvement decisions as consumers tend to put less cognitive effort in such decisions and are thus more vulnerable to acting automatically.[144] This can have both a negative and a positive effect, depending on whether the habit at issue is a sustainable one. The inhibiting role of habit on sustainable consumption was observed in several studies.[145] Nevertheless, if the established habit is a sustainable one, habitual behavior is beneficial since a once formed habit supports future sustainable actions.[146] The difficulty here, however, is the time required to establish new habits or change old ones.[147]

Besides habits, mere past experiences with a sustainable action were also found to increase the likelihood of executing it again.[148] Research even suggested that sustainable behavior in one area has the potential to leak into other areas.[149] This means that individuals who perform one type of sustainable behavior are more likely to engage in another type as well.[150] This so-called 'spillover-effect' is found to be only of moderate size and contingent on how closely the behaviors are associated in a consumer's mind.[151] For instance, low-involvement consumption

---

[140] Cf. Welsch and Kühling (2009), p.173.
[141] Cf. Steg and Vlek (2009), p.312.
[142] Cf. Verplanken and Wood (2006), p.93.
[143] Cf. Carrington et al. (2010), p.144; Yeow, Dean, and Tucker (2014), p.97.
[144] Cf. J. Davies et al. (2002), p.70; Tarkiainen and Sundqvist (2009), p.858f; W. Young, Hwang, McDonald, and Oates (2010), p.26; Torma, Aschemann-Witzel, and Thøgersen (2018), p.143.
[145] Cf. Thøgersen (1994), p. 259; Jansson, Marell, and Nordlund (2010), p.365; W. Young et al. (2010), p.26; Bray et al. (2011), p.601; Wiederhold and Martinez (2018), p.425; Hiller and Woodall (2019), p.902.
[146] Cf. Welsch and Kühling (2009), p.173; Russell et al. (2017), p.12; Wang et al. (2018), p.177.
[147] Cf. Thøgersen (1994), p.159; Verplanken and Wood (2006), p.100.
[148] Cf. Vassallo, Scalvedi, and Saba (2016), p.430; Carfora et al. (2019), p.6.
[149] Cf. Thøgersen and Ölander (2003), p.234.
[150] Thøgersen and Ölander (2003), p.234; Tilikidou and Delistavrou (2008), p.72; Barbarossa and Pelsmacker (2016), p.241; Romani, Grappi, and Bagozzi (2016), p.262.
[151] Cf. Thøgersen and Ölander (2003), p.234.

practices were not found to spill-over to high-involvement behaviors.[152] Habit is expected to be a reason for this limited effect as it decreases the likelihood that behaving sustainably in one area makes the consumer reflect on their behaviors in other domains.[153] Another line of reasoning is provided by Phipps et al. (2013), who suggest that a licensing effect, which was observed in studies conducted in similar fields, could occur in sustainable consumption too. This effect describes a phenomenon where individuals who consume sustainably do the opposite later on as they treat the previous sustainable behavior as an excuse.[154] One study already points to such an effect as they identified a few negative cross-lagged effects between buying organic food and recycling. This can be viewed as an indicator that the performance of a sustainable action reduces the propensity to behave sustainably in other areas.[155]

However, there are two techniques to limit the negative power of habits and turn them into drivers for sustainable consumption. Firstly, habits can be changed by small triggers at the point of behavior implementation. For instance, a sign which reads a request to only use one paper towel to dry one's hands lead to a significant reduction in towel use among participants of a study.[156] Nevertheless, it was also observed that when participants are faced with threatening prospects about the future and personal fallout thereof, they fall back into their environmentally harmful habits, even when these are in fact normatively inconsistent.[157] This already gives an indication that how a message is framed plays an important role, which will be discussed as part of chapter 4.2.2. Secondly, the formation of implementation intentions by the consumer, i.e. an if-then plan that describes when, where and how their intentions will be realized as actual behavior,[158] can help individuals to change their habits to more sustainable ones.[159] In case of purchasing responsibly,

---

[152] Cf. Moraes, Carrigan, Bosangit, Ferreira, and McGrath (2017), p.531.
[153] Cf. Thøgersen and Ölander (2003), p.234.
[154] Cf. Phipps et al. (2013), p.1229.
[155] Cf. Thøgersen and Ölander (2003), p.234.
[156] Cf. Buttlar et al. (2017), p.156.
[157] Cf. Buttlar et al. (2017), p.159.
[158] Cf. Gollwitzer and Sheeran (2006), p.82.
[159] Cf. Carrington, Neville, and Whitwell (2014), p.2764; Grimmer, Kilburn, and Miles (2016), p.1585;

for instance, forming plans helps not only to limit the influence of habitually buying non-sustainable products but also to resist spontaneous purchases.[160]

Both emotions and habits are powerful in guiding consumers' behaviors and also contribute to the attitude-behavior gap.[161] It was found that the attitude-behavior link is stronger when habits are weak or absent[162] and that emotions can override expressed attitudes.[163]

4.1.4 Cognitive factors

In contrast to the previous cluster, this one comprises factors that involve intellectual activity of the consumer.

Awareness, knowledge and concern

Although a study showed that subjects who were aware of the consequences their behavior has acted more responsibly,[164] most researchers are in agreement that only a small part of sustainable behavior can be directly linked to awareness.[165]

A concept closely tied to and difficult to clearly distinguish from awareness is environmental knowledge. In some cases, it has been conceptualized as a subcategory of environmental awareness.[166] While some studies showed a positive relation between knowledge and sustainable actions,[167] others came to the conclusion that knowledge only plays a minor role.[168] This inconsistency might be attributed to the different operationalizations and interpretations of knowledge in the context of sustainable consumption. It either covers knowing definitions, causes or consequences of environmental and social problems (factual knowledge) or being familiar with how to take action on them (action-related knowledge or task-specific knowledge).[169] In contrast to factual knowledge, action-related knowledge is more

---

[160] Cf. Carrington et al. (2014), p.2764.
[161] Cf. Gregory-Smith et al. (2013), p.1202; Carfora et al. (2019), p.6.
[162] Cf. Verplanken et al. (1994), p.296; Carfora et al. (2019), p.6.
[163] Cf. Gregory-Smith et al. (2013), p.1202.
[164] Cf. Buerke et al. (2016), p.979.
[165] Cf. Kollmuss and Agyeman (2002), p.250.
[166] Cf. Grob (1995), p.209; Kollmuss and Agyeman (2002), p.248.
[167] Cf. Hines et al. (1987), p.3; Tanner and Wölfing Kast (2003), p.893; Mostafa (2007), p.460.
[168] Cf. Grob (1995), p.215, Vainio and Paloniemi (2014), p.25.
[169] Cf. Hines et al. (1987), p.3; Tanner and Wölfing Kast (2003), p.886.

likely to have an impact on behavior.[170] It refers, for instance, to the ability to distinguish sustainable products from the less environmentally friendly ones. This was found to be a driving factor of responsible purchasing,[171] whereas a lack of this ability represented an inhibitor.[172] A study on the reasons for never buying green products showed that 70% of respondents lack understanding of the scope of green products and their characteristics and do not buy them as a consequence.[173] Hence, the dearth of knowledge about how to perform a particular sustainable behavior or what the most sustainable action in which to engage in is, represents an important barrier to its adoption.[174] However, this is a problem that can, in some cases, not simply be solved by the acquisition of more information. Longo et al. (2019) revealed the contrasting and paradoxical role knowledge plays in sustainable consumption. They discovered that having great knowledge can also be a source of dilemma, tension and paralysis and can thus disempower consumers in their choice to consume sustainably. For example, combining both social and environmental principles in one single purchasing option can be challenging since there exist trade-offs between these two dimensions (e.g. fair-trade wine from a distant country vs. a non-fair-trade one from a local vineyard). Moreover, knowledge can contribute to feeling inescapably trapped in unsustainable practices, which may cause tension for the individual.[175] This finding also indicates that the dysfunctional nature of consumer knowledge may partly be a result of the impacts caused by information overload and complexity common in the present times.[176]

There is one last interesting discovery concerning consumers' knowledge. Information on the sustainability of products or services is sometimes willfully ignored in order to avoid negative emotions when making unethical consumption decisions. A study found that respondents who cared about the underlying ethical issue

---

[170] Cf. Tanner and Wölfing Kast (2003), p.886.
[171] Cf. Shaw and Clarke (1999), p.115; De Pelsmacker and Janssens (2007), p.374; D'Astous and Legendre (2009), p.263; W. Young et al. (2010), p.29; Moraes et al. (2017), p.535.
[172] Cf. Shaw and Clarke (1999), p.155; Bray et al. (2011), p.602; Papaoikonomou, Ryan, and Ginieis (2011), p.83; P.-C. Lin and Huang (2012), p.16; Gabler, Butler, and Adams (2013), p.168; Gleim, Smith, Andrews, and Cronin (2013), p.57; Eberhart and Naderer (2017), p.1163.
[173] Cf. P.-C. Lin and Huang (2012), p.16.
[174] Cf. Thøgersen (1994), p.145; Tanner and Wölfing Kast (2003), p.893; Longo, Shankar, and Nuttall (2019), p.762.
[175] Cf. Shaw and Clarke (1999), p.113; Longo et al. (2019), p.769ff..
[176] Cf. Carrigan and Attalla (2001), p.573; Bray et al. (2011), p.602; Longo et al. (2019), p.762.

were the least likely to request and use environmental attribute information when they made their purchase decisions so that they can justify their unethical purchase by defensively claiming ignorance.[177]

A concept that shares commonalities with awareness and knowledge is concern, whereby the most important distinguishing factor is said to be the association of concern to emotions. While environmental knowledge is more about the cold facts of environmental problems, environmental concern brings about feelings of personal involvement and thus marks a step forward from merely being aware.[178] Although the two constructs are distinct from one another and people can be concerned with issues they have incomplete or no knowledge about,[179] they are positively correlated.[180] In terms of environmental concern being a driver for sustainable behavior, studies delivered mixed results, with some claiming it is an important driver,[181] while others did not see concern translating into behavior.[182] Inconsistent findings may be grounded in the different interpretations of the term and measurement scales used. Environmental concern is not simply ranging from low to high but is a multi-dimensional construct (concern for the self, other people or the biosphere), and it can either refer to a specific issue or to the environment in general.[183] As mentioned above in terms of general and specific attitudes, the specificity of the concern also determines its influence. It should be viewed as an important indirect rather than a direct driver of specific behavior.[184] It was argued that there are variables mediating the relationship between concern and behavior (e.g. perceived marketplace influence, see below), indicating that concern may be a necessary but not a sufficient requirement for engagement in sustainable consumption.[185]

---

[177] Cf. Ehrich and Irwin (2005), p.175f.
[178] Cf. Vainio and Paloniemi (2014), p.25.
[179] Cf. Pagiaslis and Krontalis (2014), p.346.
[180] Cf. Chai, Bradley, Lo, and Reser (2015), p.101.
[181] Cf. Kilbourne and Pickett (2008), p.891; Mobley, Vagias, and Deward (2010), p.436; P.-C. Lin and Huang (2012), p.15; Pagiaslis and Krontalis (2014), p.345; Vainio and Paloniemi (2014), p.25.
[182] Cf. Alwitt and Pitts (1996), p.60; Roberts (1996b), p.82; Mainieri, Barnett, Valdero, Unipan, and Oskamp (1997), p.200; Straughan (1999), p.570; Dermody et al. (2015), p.1485.
[183] Cf. Schultz (2000), p.397.
[184] Cf. Alwitt and Pitts (1996), p.60; Bamberg (2003), p.21.
[185] Cf. Leary, Vann, Mittelstaedt, Murphy, and Sherry (2014), p.1596.

Sense of personal responsibility

Another factor that drives sustainable consumption acts is a heightened sense of personal responsibility for environmental or social problems.[186] This is also reflected by the NAT as it views the denial of responsibility as restricting the emergence of personal norms that guide behavior.[187] The inhibiting role of denial of responsibility on behavior was empirically found to be true by researchers.[188] One argument for not feeling personally responsible is the reliance on institutions to take care of such issues (see also Appendix B).[189]

Perceived Consumer Effectiveness (PCE)

A concept very similar to the above mentioned locus of control is a consumer's perceived effectiveness (or efficacy) of consumption decisions, which is domain-specific and refers to the context of consumerism in particular.[190] It describes to what degree a consumer believes that their personal efforts can have an impact on the environment,[191] and it is similar to the concept of self-efficacy (SE). The same set of beliefs is measured in this context by some researchers,[192] although SE is more concerned with the ability to perform a task rather than influencing the underlying outcome.[193] As intuition suggests, PCE/SE promotes sustainable consumption, or its absence inhibits it, a phenomenon that has been empirically proven by numerous researchers.[194] Furthermore, PCE is enhanced by guilt and pride as discussed above.[195]

PCE is not to be confused with PBC, although not all studies make a clear distinction between these two.[196] As PBC is one of the key components of the TPB, it has proven

---

[186] Cf. Tilikidou and Delistavrou (2008), p.72; Luchs, Phipps, and Hill (2015), p.1455.
[187] Cf. Schwartz (1977), p.230.
[188] Cf. Blake (1999), p.266; Lorenzoni et al. (2007), p.452.
[189] Cf. Eckhardt, Belk, and Devinney (2010), p.431.
[190] Cf. Hines et al. (1987), p.4f.; Ellen, Wiener, and Cobb-Walgren (1991), p.103.
[191] Cf. Park and Lin (2018), p.2.
[192] Cf. Rice (2006), p.375; Hanss and Böhm (2013), p.55.
[193] Cf. Bandura (1977), p.193.
[194] Cf. Webster (1975), p.195; Roberts (1996a), p.224; Straughan (1999), p.570; Rowlands et al. (2003), p.45; Webb, Mohr, and Harris (2008), p.97; Shruti Gupta and Ogden (2009),p.386; Gabler et al. (2013), p.165; H.-Y. Lin and Hsu (2015), p.336; Wiederhold and Martinez (2018), p.426; Joshi and Rahman (2019), p.241.
[195] Cf. Antonetti and Maklan (2014), p.129.
[196] See, for example Gabler et al. (2013), p.161.

to be an important driver of sustainable behavior or a barrier in case of its absence by numerous studies.[197]

Another concept related to agency and thus similar in nature to PCE is the perceived marketplace influence, defined as the belief that the own sustainable actions actively influence the marketplace behavior of other consumers and organizations. The belief in marketplace influence was revealed to play a crucial role in transforming a consumer's environmental concern into actual actions, as mentioned above.[198]

Perceived lack of urgency and advantageousness

The last factor is not of the same level of concreteness as the ones mentioned above, but it can still be a reason why consumers do not act in a sustainable manner. The elusive nature of sustainability can lead to the unfavorable perception that sustainable actions are not urgent or advantageous. The consequences of sustainable behavior lie in the future and are uncertain, abstract and difficult for the consumers to grasp.[199] Furthermore, these consequences may merely be indirect, which promotes doubts about the effectiveness and thus negatively influences the implementation of behavior.[200] What also contributes to the inability to realize the necessity of sustainability is that consumers have not experienced the negative consequences of unsustainable actions first-hand.[201] An exploratory study found that when individuals were personally affected by an environmental problem, they were more likely to change their behavior in a more sustainable direction. The same was true when current news forced informants to contemplate about a negative issue, indicating that they were thereby reminded of the urgency to act.[202] The role of personal affectedness on behavior was confirmed by a quantitative study, where the subjects behaved more environmentally friendly when they were emotionally affected by the damage to the environment.[203]

---

[197] Cf. Bamberg and Möser (2007), p.20.
[198] Cf. Leary et al. (2014), p.1597.
[199] Cf. McCarty and Shrum (2001), p.93; Spence, Poortinga, and Pidgeon (2012), p.7ff.; Trudel (2018), p.88.
[200] Cf. Eberhart and Naderer (2017), p.1163.
[201] Cf. Ozaki (2011), p.13; M. L. Johnstone and Tan (2015), p.320; Eberhart and Naderer (2017), p.1162.
[202] Cf. Bray et al. (2011), p.601f..
[203] Cf. Grob (1995), p.215.

4.2 Environmental factors

The second major category describes external forces from the environment of the consumer that have an influence on their sustainable consumption behaviors in either a positive or negative respect. The three behavioral theories explained above do not include such contextual factors sufficiently. The construct of PBC, as included in the TPB, merely captures the individuals' perceptions of contextual factors.[204] The identified environmental factors can be divided into four clusters: product, service or behavior-related factors, corporate activities, social influence and structural conditions. All are subsequently discussed.

4.2.1 Product, service or behavior-related factors

This cluster includes determinants that stem from the sustainable product or service per se or the implementation of a particular sustainable behavior, which is why they do not apply to every sustainable consumption act.

Cost of consumption

Price is a factor that is particularly present when purchasing sustainable products or services and is proving to be a controversial issue. While consumers commonly state that the higher prices of sustainable products or services inhibit their consumption,[205] **some studies showed that it is not a barrier.**[206] **Thus, it was argued that price is not an obstacle per se, but it arises as one when consumers are financially constrained**[207] **or if they are particularly price sensitive**[208]. This was proven by a qualitative study, which found that consumers experiencing economic difficulties more frequently mention price as a barrier.[209] **This indicates an intersection of the environmental factor price with the individual's perception about whether the higher price for a sustainable product or service is justified or not. The perception of consumers about the economic**

---

[204] Cf. Steg and Vlek (2009), p.312.
[205] Cf. Carrigan and Attalla (2001), p.569; Hunecke et al. (2001), p.845; Bray et al. (2011), p.601; Ozaki (2011), p.11; Öberseder, Schlegelmilch, and Gruber (2011), p.455; Papaoikonomou et al. (2011), p.84; Gleim et al. (2013), p.52; Han, Seo, and Ko (2017), p.165; Papista, Chrysochou, Krystallis, and Dimitriadis (2018), p.108; Wiederhold and Martinez (2018);
[206] Cf. Thøgersen (1994), p.159; Tanner and Wölfing Kast (2003), p.893; P.-C. Lin and Huang (2012), p.17.
[207] Cf. Cherrier, Szuba, and Özçağlar-Toulouse (2012), p.13; Valor and Carrero (2014), p.1115.
[208] Cf. Gleim et al. (2013), p.52; M. Janssen (2018), p.26.
[209] Cf. Valor and Carrero (2014), p.1115.

profitability of sustainable products was shown to be disadvantageous. **Some consumer assume that sustainable products are generally more expensive than** 'regular' ones and therefore infer that they will not be able to afford them, even when this is, in fact, not always true.[210] **Others do not take into account future cost savings that sustainable products with an initially higher price provide.**[211] A reason for this unfavorable perception is that in some consumers' minds, ethics and business are two separate dimensions and they therefore assume that sustainable practices must involve higher costs.[212]

Besides the monetary costs, **there are other resources a person has to spend on the consumption, such as the time and effort needed throughout the whole consumption cycle. The higher amount of effort needed to engage in the sustainable behavior and the inconvenience this entails is naturally a barrier to its adoption.**[213] **Again, it depends not only on the objective costs of engaging in the behavior but also the perception of the individual's personal inconvenience** involved.[214] **Other decisive factors are the amount of time engaging in a sustainable behavior requires and how much time an individual has at one's disposal.**[215] **It was shown that a lack of discretionary time prevents consumers from developing preferences that are in line with their underlying environmental concerns, and an increase in discretionary time enhances sustainable consumption behaviors and also reduces the attitude-behavior gap.**[216]

A less researched topic is the cost involved in changing from one product, service or behavior to another one, so-called switching costs, such as search effort or performance risk.[217] While one study on this topic found no significant effect of switching costs on customer value,[218] **another one revealed that the inconvenience of**

---

[210] Cf. Öberseder et al. (2011), p.455.
[211] Cf. Gleim et al. (2013), p.46.
[212] Cf. I. Davies et al. (2012), p.45.
[213] Cf. Carrigan and Attalla (2001), p.570; McCarty and Shrum (2001), p.101; Tilikidou and Delistavrou (2008), p.69; W. Young et al. (2010), p.26; Gleim et al. (2013), p.48; Barbarossa and Pelsmacker (2016), p.240; M. L. Johnstone and Tan (2015), p.316; Papista et al. (2018), p.108.
[214] Cf. Barbarossa and Pelsmacker (2016), p.239.
[215] Cf. Carrigan and Attalla (2001), p.573; Tanner and Wölfing Kast (2003), p.893; W. Young et al. (2010), p.25.
[216] Cf. Chai et al. (2015), p.105.
[217] Cf. Papista et al. (2018), p.108.
[218] Cf. Papista et al. (2018), p.108.

switching to a green energy tariff and uncertainty about its performance is a barrier to its adoption.[219]

While cost of consumption is often mentioned in the reviewed literature, hardly any benefits connected to the sustainability of consumption occur. The exception to this is the enjoyment consumers find in repurposing products.[220]

Performance, stereotypes and image

The issue with the quality of sustainable products and services varies among different categories and is very intricate. Firstly, despite a few respondents commenting on the better quality of sustainable products, for instance in terms of naturalness and healthiness of organic food or clothing,[221] others stated perceptions of lesser quality,[222] e.g. with regard to the design of clothing[223] or effectiveness of cleaning products.[224]

The latter might be explained by the following finding: Sustainable products are associated with gentleness-related attributes by consumers, while less sustainable alternatives are associated with strength-related attributes.[225] This effect of gentleness works against perceptions of effectiveness and competence, and as a consequence, sustainability is found to be unfavorable when consumers are looking for strength-related products (i.e., where benefits such as power and durability are in the foreground, like for cleaning products). In contrast, when gentle attributes (e.g. baby shampoo) are searched for, consumers prefer sustainable products. This shows that the product category, or more precisely the related degree to which strength is valued in a given category, determines if negative product quality impressions are triggered and thus whether the sustainability of the product is seen as advantageous or not.[226] An implicitly or explicitly held negative perception decreases the likelihood of purchasing sustainable products.[227] It also results in an

---

[219] Cf. Ozaki (2011), p.9ff..
[220] Scott and Weaver (2018), p.303.
[221] Cf. Bray et al. (2011), p.602; Thøgersen and Zhou (2012), p.327; M. Janssen (2018), p.26.
[222] Cf. Bray et al. (2011), p.602; Y.-C. Lin and Chang (2012), p.133; Newman, Gorlin, and Dhar (2014), p.834; Eberhart and Naderer (2017), p.1163; Han et al. (2017), p.165; Wiederhold and Martinez (2018), p.424; Kushwah et al. (2019), p.10.
[223] Cf. Wiederhold and Martinez (2018), p.426.
[224] Cf. Y.-C. Lin and Chang (2012), p.133.
[225] Cf. Luchs et al. (2010), p.21.
[226] Cf. Luchs et al. (2010), p.22ff..
[227] Cf. Mai, Hoffmann, Lasarov, and Buhs (2019), p.672.

increase of the amount of sustainable product used to gain a desired result, for instance to make something clean.[228] While one study found that environmentally conscious consumers are more likely to display this usage pattern,[229] another one showed that increased interest in sustainability can reduce the negative perception of a sustainable product, albeit the implicit negative associations remain.[230] Moreover, this study observed that consumers are more likely to opt for the conventional instead of the sustainable option in case of impulse choices or in case the consumers are unobserved.[231] This supports the prior discussed finding that low-involvement or habitual behavior is more prone to unsustainability and indicates that the visibility of actions might have an influence (see also below). Interestingly, even the presence of very fundamental human needs, such as hunger, were found to affect stereotypical perceptions of sustainable products in a negative way. Food deprivation unconsciously alters the implicit associations concerning sustainability, i.e. the products' gentleness, and consequently leads to less sustainable purchase decisions.[232]

As with the previously stated assumption that sustainability comes with higher costs, consumers were also found to have the impression that sustainability must be compensated by inferiority in other dimensions such as the product's quality, especially when companies *deliberately* consider sustainability aspects in their products in order to enhance them.[233] Once again, this highlights the intersection of external stimuli and the perceptions of the individual.

Apart from the stereotype that sustainable products are less strong and effective, there also exists the stereotype that being environmentally friendly is unmanly.[234] This often keeps men from buying sustainable products as they want to preserve their gender identity.[235] In addition, it was recognized that users of responsible brands are perceived as stereotypically warm, which diminishes feelings of envy and weakens the desire to emulate such consumers.[236] Another study discovered

---

[228] Cf. Y.-C. Lin and Chang (2012), p.132.
[229] Cf. Y.-C. Lin and Chang (2012), p.132.
[230] Cf. Mai et al. (2019), p.669.
[231] Cf. Mai et al. (2019), p.671.
[232] Cf. Hoffmann, Mai, Lasarov, Krause, and Schmidt (2019), p.100f.
[233] Cf. Newman et al. (2014), p.834.
[234] Cf. Shang and Peloza (2015), p.140; Brough et al. (2016), p.579.
[235] Cf. Brough et al. (2016), p.579.
[236] Cf. Antonetti and Maklan (2016), p.797.

that consumers generally have an unfavorable perception of sustainable consumers, also called social-stigma, which prevents consumers from engaging in such behaviors.[237] This points to the importance of social influence, further discussed below. However, as with almost all determinants so far, this one does not come without contradictions: With regard to organic food, Kushwah et al. (2019) could not find evidence for an image barrier.[238]

4.2.2 Corporate activities

While companies or institutions cannot eliminate the information overload, whose negative effect on knowledge is discussed above, they can influence how and what information they present. This is particularly important as deficient credibility was also discovered to hinder sustainable consumption.[239] However, providing credible information in an adequate amount is not a simple task. Sustainability claims and other communication on this subject, for example about a company's social responsibility, are generally approached with mistrust and skepticism.[240] This influences how consumers perceive and judge sustainable offerings and thus also their behavior.[241] Trustworthy and clear information was found as a driver for sustainable consumption and can, for example, be provided via labels. This helps to reduce the cognitive effort of a consumer's decision[242] and was found to be especially effective for low-involvement decisions where consumers are less motivated to carefully evaluate information. A sustainable appeal can then act as a prominent and easily accessible trigger to opt for the sustainable product.[243] Indeed, a more complete, easily interpretable and standardized label was observed to promote eco-friendly consumption.[244] This applies at least to the purchase of groceries, as consumers were found to use their personal networks as a source of information for higher-

---

[237] Cf. M. L. Johnstone and Tan (2015), p.319f..
[238] Cf. Kushwah et al. (2019), p.11.
[239] Cf. Papaoikonomou et al. (2011), p.83.; De Pelsmacker and Janssens (2007), p.374; Antonetti and Maklan (2014b), p.729.
[240] Cf. Bray et al. (2011), p.603; Öberseder et al. (2011), p.456; Gleim et al. (2013), p.47; Rettie, Burchell, and Barnham (2014), p.13; M. L. Johnstone and Hooper (2016), p. 824.
[241] Cf. De Pelsmacker and Janssens (2007), p.364; Bray et al. (2011), p.603; Öberseder et al. (2011), p.457.
[242] Cf. W. Young et al. (2010), p.26f..
[243] Cf. Rahman (2018), p.402.
[244] Cf. Vlaeminck, Jiang, and Vranken (2014), p.187f..

involvement decisions.[245] Furthermore, it was observed that the European government and non-governmental organizations like Greenpeace are the most trusted issuers of such labels. This shows that effective communication requires collaboration between companies and institutions.[246] Apart from this, technology and more specifically green mobile apps proved to be another method for consumers to acquire information and thereby foster sustainable purchasing.[247]

Generally, research showed that a company's communication efforts can alter consumers' behaviors in a more sustainable direction. An exemplary measure to be mentioned is that of a retailer which presented standard food waste reduction messages to its consumers via different conventional communication channels (e.g. social media and in-store demonstrations) and thereby decreased the consumers' food waste.[248] Companies should, however, be careful in their message framing as this has an effect on the consumers' reaction and in turn the behavior. While negatively framed messages are more effective than positively framed ones due to the shame it elicits in consumers,[249] too assertively phrased messages can have a negative impact on consumers' behavior, depending on the importance the message recipient attaches to the behavior at stake.[250]

Besides the fact that companies can be enablers of sustainable consumer behavior, they can also represent a reason why an individual does not consume in a sustainable manner. This is the case when brand loyalty to an unsustainable company prevents a consumer from switching to a sustainable alternative.[251] In case of small electrical appliances, for instance, it was found that the brand is given priority over sustainability criteria.[252] However, the power that companies possess in this context may offer an opportunity, as individuals might consume in a more sustainable manner if a company to which they are loyal eliminates unsustainable products and services from their assortment.

---

[245] Cf. McDonald, Oates, Thyne, Alevizou, and McMorland (2009), p.143.
[246] Cf. De Pelsmacker et al. (2005), p.524.
[247] Cf. Perera, Auger, and Klein (2018), p.850.
[248] Cf. C. W. Young, Russell, Robinson, and Chintakayala (2018), p.11ff..
[249] Cf. Amatulli, De Angelis, Peluso, Soscia, and Guido (2019), p.1125.
[250] Cf. Kronrod, Grinstein, and Wathieu (2012), p.100.
[251] Cf. Bray et al. (2011), p.605; Papaoikonomou et al. (2011), p.80; Gleim et al. (2013), p.48.
[252] Cf. McDonald et al. (2009), p.140.

4.2.3 Social influence

Much of consumption decisions are not made in isolation but also take into account the needs, desires and expectations of others, such as family members, friends, community members and even the general public.[253] How this variety of actors can impact a person's behavior is explained below.

For one thing, there is the influence on an interpersonal level that comes from close persons like family and friends.[254] The most common theme in the literature relating thereto seems to be the phenomenon of subordinating one's own sustainable intentions to the opinions or wishes of family and friends. Essentially, interacting with people that do not share one's sustainable principles and might not even show understanding for them represented an inhibitor to the pursuit of one's sustainable practices in several studies.[255] Examples of this include buying unsustainable products because one's partner enjoys them, one's children refuse to consume alternatives, or flying to a family gathering one is expected to join.[256] As already described in paragraph 2.2.2, the difference in the wishes and attitudes of close others and of one's self can contribute to the gap between attitude and behavior. However, significant others can also be a driver of sustainable consumption,[257] for instance in case of adolescents, who are found to be more inclined to act pro-environmentally when their parents visibly do so.[258]

For another thing, unrelated others, not necessarily belonging to one's group affiliation, can have an impact on a consumer's behavior.[259] This mostly takes the form of social norms, which are "unwritten rules developed through shared interactions of a social group that govern social behavior" (Trudel, 2018, p.91). Studies have demonstrated the usefulness of social norms to affect behavior across several different domains, including reusing towels in hotels[260], composting[261], reducing

---

[253] Cf. Cherrier et al. (2012), p.28; Gleim et al. (2013), p.46.
[254] Cf. Trudel (2018), p.91.
[255] Cf. Papaoikonomou et al. (2011), p.84; Szmigin et al. (2009), p.228; Cherrier et al. (2012), p.19; M. L. Johnstone and Tan (2015), p.318; McDonald et al. (2015), p.1513.
[256] Cf. Szmigin et al. (2009), p.228; Cherrier et al. (2012), p.19; Papaoikonomou et al. (2011), p.85.
[257] Cf. Yeow et al. (2014), p.91.
[258] Cf. Grønhøj and Thøgersen (2012), p.299.
[259] Cf. Trudel (2018), p.91.
[260] Cf. Goldstein, Cialdini, and Griskevicius (2008), p.479.
[261] Cf. White and Simpson (2013), p.78.

household energy consumption[262] and purchasing sustainable food[263]. Social norm was also shown to have an impact on attitude and PCB, as it is used by consumers for judgements of how easy and advantageous the performance of a specific action would be.[264] While research collectively shows the persuasive power of social norms, it is of importance to note that the success depends on what type of and how social norm is applied. The first type are descriptive norms, which describe what most people do in a situation. The second type are injunctive norms, which characterize what others think one should be doing, indicating which behaviors commonly receive approval or disapproval.[265] It is best to align these two types,[266] demonstrated by the results of the following study, which tested the effect of normative appeals on household energy reduction: The messages sent differed depending on whether the household's energy consumption was above or below average. While providing above-average households with descriptive norm information led to a decrease of consumption, the same descriptive norm information increased consumption in below-average households. However, adding an injunctive norm conveying approval of their low energy consumption eliminated this negative effect.[267] Furthermore, it was found that the effectiveness of descriptive norms also depends on the reference group mentioned in the appeal sent. It works best to refer to the norms of the consumer's local setting and circumstances. e.g. individuals that stayed in the specific hotel room before the consumer's own stay.[268] A third factor that possibly influences how strong social norm affects a consumers' behavior is whether the action at issue is visible to others and whether it is in the individual's hands only, such as saving energy or wasting food at home.[269]

Another observation worth mentioning in connection with social influence is the process of social normalization and how it shapes consumer's behavior. Rettie et al. (2014) discovered that consumers' perception of what a 'normal' behavior is influences its adoption. Consumers are reluctant to behave in a way that is not considered as 'normal' and, conversely, are more likely to engage in activities that are

---

[262] Cf. Schultz, Nolan, Cialdini, Goldstein, and Griskevicius (2007), p.432; Ozaki (2011), p.12.
[263] Cf. Gleim et al. (2013), p.53 Vermeir and Verbeke (2006), p.187.
[264] Cf. Bamberg and Möser (2007), p .22.
[265] Cf. Cialdini (2003), p.105.
[266] Cf. Cialdini (2003), p.105.
[267] Cf. Schultz et al. (2007), p.432.
[268] Cf. Goldstein et al. (2008), p. 479.
[269] Cf. Russell et al. (2017), p.108f.; Wang et al. (2018), p.178.

deemed mainstream. This contributes to understanding why some unsustainable behaviors are difficult to change: they are taken for granted and are not questioned due to the perception that they are just 'normal' and part of modern life, such as driving a car.[270]

Apart from the influence caused by family, friends or unrelated others, there is a third way by which other people can affect somebody else's sustainable behavior, this time a positive one only. Research found that online communities of likeminded consumers can reinforce sustainable consumption, especially due to informational benefits (e.g. provision of answers to common questions or sharing of practical tips and ideas on sustainable consumption).[271] From this it can be deduced that influencers who promote sustainability could drive sustainable consumer behavior in a similar vein.

4.2.4 Structural conditions

The final cluster addresses determinants over which neither the individual companies nor the consumer alone can exert influence because they deal with public policy, infrastructure and today's lifestyle. Collective action and collaboration between different stakeholders are necessary to make changes to these barriers and turn them into drivers.

It was argued that structural issues are creating a dependence on unsustainable consumption practices. It is suggested that several factors contribute toward this lock-in, including living and working conditions as well as public policy.[272] Thus, governments are responsible for part of the external circumstances that restrict a consumer's freedom of choice and action. Among them are the availability and quality of public transportation, accessibility of recycling facilities and the presence and affordability of sustainable products and services.[273] An empirical case study, for example, showed that the introduction of new recycling policies which included economic incentives had a powerful positive effect on the recycling rates of the inhabitants of the city being researched.[274] Furthermore, the lack of available

---

[270] Cf. Rettie et al. (2014), p.12ff..

[271] Cf. Gummerus, Liljander, and Sihlman (2017), p.459f..

[272] Cf. Sanne (2002), p.273; Prothero et al. (2011), p.33; Banbury, Stinerock, and Subrahmanyan (2012), p.503; Di Giulio et al. (2014), p.48.

[273] Cf. Thøgersen (2005), p.145; Press and Arnould (2009), p.105; Barr (2007), p.467; Steg and Vlek (2009), p.312; M. L. Johnstone and Hooper (2016), p.846f..

[274] Cf. Viscusi, Huber, and Bell (2011), p.70.

sustainable alternatives was often mentioned in the literature as discouraging sustainable behavior and, conversely, the availability of sustainable products and services was mentioned as encouraging it.[275] This barrier might increasingly vanish, at least with regard to sustainable groceries and clothing, as they are becoming more **widely and easily available in current times.**[276] **What is indeed regarded as an obstacle are living and working circumstances that limit the time and scope for engaging in sustainable behaviors.**[277] **The growing urbanization, for instance, may lead to longer commutes to work, which in turn results in people using their cars more intensively.**[278]

4.3 Conceptual model and additional remarks

The above described variety of influencing factors, their interconnectedness and the different consumption behaviors that can be classified as sustainable contribute to the difficulty of developing a model that incorporates all possible factors.[279] However, figure 3 depicts the main categories of the factors that could be derived from the literature. For ease of presentation, possible interplays between determinants are not shown.

---

[275] Cf. Shaw and Clarke (1999), p.115; Hira and Ferrie (2006), p.109; Vermeir and Verbeke (2008), p.547; Papaoikonomou et al. (2011), p.84; I. Davies et al. (2012), p.46; Gleim et al. (2013), p.48; Grimmer et al. (2016), p.1585; Lundblad and Davies (2016), p.157; Moraes et al. (2017), p.535.

[276] Cf. Bray et al. (2011), p.604; Lundblad and Davies (2016), p.157.

[277] Cf. Sanne (2002), p.277ff.; Chai et al. (2015), p.105.

[278] Cf. Sanne (2002), p.277.

[279] Cf. Hines et al. (1987), p.6; Kollmuss and Agyeman (2002), p.239.

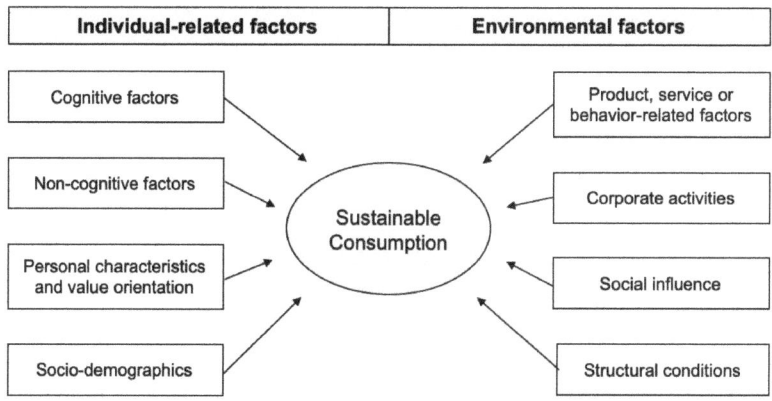

Fig. 3: The main factors that have an impact on sustainable consumption[280]

The numerous factors that have a bearing on the consumer's eventual behavior act at different stages in the process from values or beliefs to behavior.[281] After reviewing the different determinants as well as the mutual influence they have on the implementation of behavior,[282] it becomes comprehensible why consumers with positive attitudes toward sustainable actions do not always follow through and an attitude-behavior gap emerges. In addition to the determinants identified in the reviewed empirical studies, it sometimes might even be a small, momentary factor at the point of behavior implementation that inhibits or facilitates the translation of sustainable intentions into behavior.[283] Such interferences in the choice context have so far been discussed theoretically in the context of sustainable purchasing and include temporary external factors, such as the physical surrounding in a store (e.g. product placement or promotions) or the social surrounding (e.g. interaction with salespeople or presence of a shopping companion) as well as internal factors like a consumer's mood.[284]

Besides this, what is holding one person back from acting in a sustainable manner may not be an obstacle for another. Equally, a consumer's preference for sustainable behaviors varies across time and situations. A consumer that acted in a

---

[280] Own illustration on the basis of the determinants identified in the reviewed literature.
[281] Cf. Papaoikonomou et al. (2011), p. 86; C. Janssen and Vanhamme (2015), p.778.
[282] Cf. H.-Y. Lin and Hsu (2015), p.327.
[283] Cf. Carrington et al. (2010), p.147.
[284] Cf. Carrington et al. (2010), p.152ff..

sustainable manner once might not do so another day or when it comes to another behavior.[285] This irregularity was also shown to depend on the product category and the associated involvement of the consumer and purchase frequency. The literature on these differences, however, is scarce to date.[286] Apart from the ones already indicated above, there are some differences with regard to, for instance, the likelihood to resist consumption of a product (renunciation of fridge or washing machine is not considered viable while doing without meat is comparatively common)[287], purchase criteria used (prestige or self-image are additional criteria for luxury products)[288] or social influence (the effect is smaller on low-involvement behavior)[289]. This highlights again that sustainable consumption needs to be viewed in a differentiated way.

Finally, drivers and barriers of sustainable consumption are in some cases also viewed or conceptualized as determinants of the gap between attitude and sustainable consumption behavior,[290] as suggested in chapter 2.2.2 above. Hence, figure 4 below not only gives a more detailed outline of the identified drivers and barriers but also marks which of them is said to contribute to the gap in the reviewed articles, denoted by a red (green) background in case the determinant increases (reduces) the attitude-behavior gap.

---

[285] Cf. Roberts and Bacon (1997), p.81; Papaoikonomou et al. (2011), p.79; McDonald et al. (2009), p.141; Szmigin et al. (2009), p.229.

[286] Cf. Jansson et al. (2010), p.358; McDonald et al. (2009), p.143; Welsch and Kühling (2009), p.173; Prothero et al. (2011), p.33; I. Davies et al. (2012), p.37; Rahman (2018), p.400; Trudel (2018), p.93.

[287] Cf. McDonald et al. (2009), p.142.

[288] Cf. I. Davies et al. (2012), p.47.

[289] Cf. Shaw and Shiu (2003), p.1492; De Pelsmacker and Janssens (2007), p.364.

[290] See, for instance, Wiederhold and Martinez (2018), p.424.

Drivers and barriers of sustainable consumption

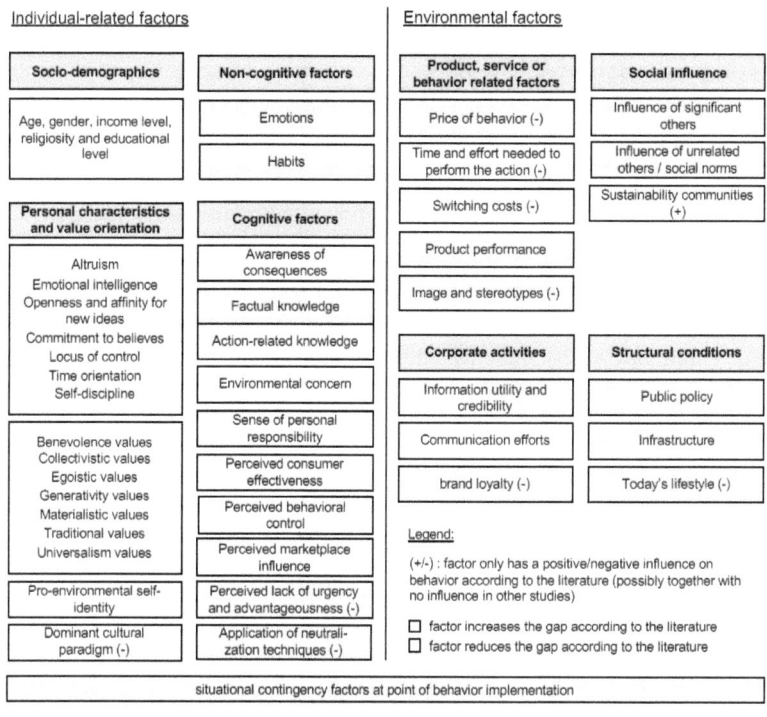

Fig. 4: More detailed representation of the drivers and barriers of sustainable consumption as well as factors influencing the attitude-behavior gap[291]

---

[291] Own illustration on the basis of the determinants identified in the reviewed literature.

5 Implications and future research

As the previous chapter makes clear, there exists no ultimate way to promote a sustainable behavior or to close the attitude-behavior gap due to the variety and otherness of factors that have an impact. Thus, a combination of different instruments adapted to the specific type of consumption act is required.[292] Generally, a mixture of informational strategies, i.e. altering individual-related factors like perceptions or knowledge and structural strategies aimed at changing the external circumstances in which choices are made is useful.[293] Informational strategies include but are not limited to social support and role models, since solely informing consumers was found not to be effective.[294] This was also demonstrated above by the knowledge dilemma and the great influence that social norms proved to have. Structural strategies like increasing the quality of the public transportation system enhance individual opportunities to act sustainably and make this behavior more attractive. It also indirectly impacts individual-related factors in that it makes, for instance, an individual's attitude toward a specific sustainable behavior more favorable.[295] Equally, marketers of sustainable products or services should tailor their strategy to their respective offering.[296] Thus, an important step is to assess the factors that inhibit or drive the adoption of the product or service at stake.[297] The determinants identified above provide a good overview of possible factors. For instance, when promoting a sustainable product where strength attributes are important, the effectiveness should clearly and credibly be highlighted to counteract negative stereotypes.[298] Besides appropriate labels, in-store demonstrations can be helpful to meet consumer's information needs in this respect and also to assist consumers in distinguishing sustainable products from unsustainable ones – an important aforementioned barrier.

Moreover, the literature review revealed several avenues for future research. Firstly, as research so far has focused on low-involvement behaviors (e.g. buying

---

[292] Cf. Di Giulio et al. (2014), p.56.
[293] Cf. Thøgersen (1994), p.159; Steg and Vlek (2009), p.313.
[294] Cf. Abrahamse, Steg, Vlek, and Rothengatter (2005), p.281; Steg and Vlek (2009), p.313.
[295] Cf. Steg and Vlek (2009), p.313.
[296] Cf. Rahman (2018), p.411.
[297] Cf. Abrahamse et al. (2005), p.283.
[298] Cf. Y.-C. Lin and Chang (2012), p.133.

sustainable groceries),[299] there is a scarcity of articles dealing with high-involvement and infrequent behaviors (e.g. installing solar panels). However, these are of great importance as they also have a large impact on the environment.[300] More work on this and comparisons between low and high involvement decisions as well as utilitarian and hedonic products and services is needed. Secondly, since the focus of researchers has lied on the purchasing phase of the consumption cycle or the act of recycling,[301] behaviors in other stages of the consumption cycle or anti-consumption and associated phenomena such as voluntary simplicity or re-usage have been rarely studied so far.[302] Reduced consumption might be of special interest as such behavior is difficult to encourage[303] and can presumably make a major contribution to the world's sustainable development. Thirdly, the articles published so far almost exclusively examine purchasing products and not the utilization of services. The latter might therefore be another interesting area for future research. Furthermore, cross-country comparisons are rare,[304] which is why culture and other local differences particularities[305] is another suggested direction for future research. In addition to this, there exists little research on the role of purchase situations and momentary factors in general that might have an influence on the consumer's behavior.[306] Finally yet importantly, future research might consider methods such as ethnography and actual data rather than the current primarily used instrument of self-reporting, which is prone to widening the attitude-behavior gap.[307]

---

[299] Cf. Jansson et al. (2010), p358; Prothero et al. (2011), p.33; Rahman (2018), p.400.
[300] Cf. Trudel (2018), p.93.
[301] Cf. Tilikidou and Delistavrou (2008), p.61.
[302] Cf. Prothero et al. (2011), p.32.
[303] Cf. Barr (2007), p.470.
[304] Cf. Newholm and Shaw (2007) ,p.264; an exception is Bucic, Harris, and Arli (2012), p.113.
[305] Cf. Bucic et al. (2012), p.129.
[306] Cf. Carrington et al. (2010), p.155; Grimmer et al. (2016), p.1583.
[307] Cf. M. Janssen (2018), p.20; Govind et al. (2019), p.1198.

6 Conclusion

The investigation of the drivers and barriers shows that sustainable consumption is complex, multi-faceted and depends on the consumer's circumstances[308] – both the physical and social ones.[309] Thus, for predicting and promoting such behavior an integrated approach is required and the consideration of different variables or measures respectively is necessary.[310] With regard to the growing popularity of sustainability in people's everyday lives, as demonstrated by the Fridays for Future movement or the recent obligation for large businesses to disclose a sustainability report[311], it can be assumed that the reasons why an individual consumes sustainably are exposed to changes in the future. While new reasons might emerge, others are omitted. It may be, for example, that the prevailing perception of consuming sustainably shifts from not normal and unfavorable[312] to trendy and worth aspiring for. Another reasonable presumption is that sustainable acts will be incentivized by governments or new sustainable business models will simply be the better alternative for consumers. This highlights that businesses can play a crucial role in the consumption patterns of individuals, which gives them the opportunity to change these. An essential step to influencing consumers is understanding them. The present thesis will hopefully make a small contribution to this end.

---

[308] Cf. Nair and Little (2016), p.181f.
[309] Cf. Carrington et al. (2010), p.147.
[310] Cf. Ertz et al. (2016), p.3974.
[311] Cf. European Commission (2014), p.4
[312] Cf. Rettie et al. (2014), p.9; M. L. Johnstone and Tan (2015), p.319.

Bibliography

Abdulrazak, & Quoquab. (2018). Exploring Consumers' Motivations for Sustainable Consumption: A Self-Deterministic Approach. *Journal of International Consumer Marketing, 30*(1), 14-28. doi:10.1080/08961530.2017.1354350

Abrahamse, Steg, Vlek, & Rothengatter. (2005). A Review of Intervention Studies Aimed at Household Energy Conservation. *Journal of Environmental Psychology, 25*(3), 273-291. doi:10.1016/j.jenvp.2005.08.002

Ajzen. (1991). The theory of planned behavior. *Organizational Behavior and Human Decision Processes, 50*(2), 179-211. doi:https://doi.org/10.1016/0749-5978(91)90020-T

Ajzen. (2002). Perceived Behavioral Control, Self-Efficacy, Locus of Control, and the Theory of Planned Behavior. *Journal of Applied Social Psychology, 32*(4), 665-683. doi:10.1111/j.1559-1816.2002.tb00236.x

Ajzen. (2011). The theory of planned behaviour: Reactions and reflections. *Psychology & Health, 26*(9), 1113-1127. doi:10.1080/08870446.2011.613995

Ajzen, & Fishbein. (1980). *Understanding Attitudes and Predicting Social Behaviour*. Englewood-Cliffs, NJ.: Prentice-Hall.

Ajzen, & Fishbein. (2000). Attitudes and the Attitude-Behavior Relation: Reasoned and Automatic Processes. *European Review of Social Psychology, 11*(1), 1-33. doi:10.1080/14792779943000116

Ajzen, & Fishbein. (2005). The Influence of Attitudes on Behavior. In *The handbook of attitudes.* (pp. 173-221). Mahwah, NJ, US: Lawrence Erlbaum Associates Publishers.

Alwitt, & Pitts. (1996). Predicting Purchase Intentions for an Environmentally Sensitive Product. *Journal of Consumer Psychology, 5*(1), 49-64. doi:10.1207/s15327663jcp0501_03

Amatulli, De Angelis, Peluso, Soscia, & Guido. (2019). The Effect of Negative Message Framing on Green Consumption: An Investigation of the Role of Shame. *Journal of Business Ethics, 157*(4), 1111-1132. doi:10.1007/s10551-017-3644-x

Bibliography

Antonetti, & Maklan. (2014). Feelings that make a difference: How guilt and pride convince consumers of the effectiveness of sustainable consumption choices. *Journal of Business Ethics, 124*(1), 117-134. doi:10.1007/s10551-013-1841-9

Antonetti, & Maklan. (2014b). Exploring Postconsumption Guilt and Pride in the Context of Sustainability. *Psychology & Marketing, 31*(9), 717-735. doi:10.1002/mar.20730

Antonetti, & Maklan. (2016). Hippies, Greenies, and Tree Huggers: How the "Warmth" Stereotype Hinders the Adoption of Responsible Brands. *Psychology & Marketing, 33*(10), 796-813. doi:10.1002/mar.20918

Assadourian. (2010). Transforming Cultures: From Consumerism to Sustainability. *Journal of Macromarketing, 30*(2), 186-191. doi:10.1177/0276146710361932

Auger, & Devinney. (2007). Do What Consumers Say Matter? The Misalignment of Preferences with Unconstrained Ethical Intentions. *Journal of Business Ethics, 76*(4), 361-383. doi:10.1007/s10551-006-9287-y

Balderjahn, Buerke, Kirchgeorg, Peyer, Seegebarth, & Wiedmann. (2013). Consciousness for sustainable consumption: scale development and new insights in the economic dimension of consumers' sustainability. *AMS Review, 3*(4), 181-192. doi:10.1007/s13162-013-0057-6

Bamberg. (2003). How Does Environmental Concern Influence Specific Environmentally Related Behaviors? A New Answer to an Old Question. *Journal of Environmental Psychology, 23*(1), 21-32. doi:10.1016/S0272-4944(02)00078-6

Bamberg, & Möser. (2007). Twenty years after Hines, Hungerford, and Tomera: A new meta-analysis of psycho-social determinants of pro-environmental behaviour. *Journal of Environmental Psychology, 27*(1), 14-25. doi:10.1016/j.jenvp.2006.12.002

Banbury, Stinerock, & Subrahmanyan. (2012). Sustainable consumption: Introspecting across multiple lived cultures. *Journal of Business Research, 65*(4), 497-503. doi:https://doi.org/10.1016/j.jbusres.2011.02.028

Bandura. (1977). Self-efficacy: Toward a unifying theory of behavioral change. *Psychological Review, 84*(2), 191-215. doi:10.1037/0033-295X.84.2.191

Barbarossa, & Pelsmacker. (2016). Positive and Negative Antecedents of Purchasing Eco-friendly Products: A Comparison Between Green and Non-green Consumers. *Journal of Business Ethics, 134*(2), 229-247. doi:10.1007/s10551-014-2425-z

Barr. (2007). Factors Influencing Environmental Attitudes and Behaviors. *Environment and Behavior, 39*(4), 435-473. doi:10.1177/0013916505283421

Bateman, & Valentine. (2010). Investigating the Effects of Gender on Consumers' Moral Philosophies and Ethical Intentions. *Journal of Business Ethics, 95*(3), 393-414.

Blake. (1999). Overcoming the 'value-action gap' in environmental policy: Tensions between national policy and local experience. *Local Environment, 4*(3), 257-278. doi:10.1080/13549839908725599

Boulstridge, & Carrigan. (2000). Do consumers really care about corporate responsibility? Highlighting the attitude—behaviour gap. *Journal of Communication Management, 4*(4), 355-368. doi:10.1108/eb023532

Bové, D'Herde, Swartz, Dempsey, Rosenfield, Seiler, & Tsui. (2017). Sustainability's deepening imprint. Retrieved from https://www.mckinsey.com/business-functions/sustainability/our-insights/sustainabilitys-deepening-imprint

Bray, Johns, & Kilburn. (2011). An Exploratory Study into the Factors Impeding Ethical Consumption. *Journal of Business Ethics, 98*(4), 597-608. doi:10.1007/s10551-010-0640-9

British Broadcasting Corporation. (2019). Global climate strikes: Millions of children take part in protests to help protect the planet. *BBC newsround*. Retrieved from https://www.bbc.co.uk/newsround/49766020

Brough, Wilkie, Jingjing, Isaac, & Gal. (2016). Is Eco-Friendly Unmanly? The Green-Feminine Stereotype and Its Effect on Sustainable Consumption. *Journal of Consumer Research, 43*(4), 567-582. doi:10.1093/jcr/ucw044

Bucic, Harris, & Arli. (2012). Ethical Consumers Among the Millennials: A Cross-National Study. *Journal of Business Ethics, 110*(1), 113-131. doi:10.1007/s10551-011-1151-z

Buerke, Straatmann, Lin-Hi, & Müller. (2016). Consumer awareness and sustainability-focused value orientation as motivating factors of responsible consumer behavior. *Review of Managerial Science, 11*(4). doi:10.1007/s11846-016-0211-2

Buttlar, Latz, & Walther. (2017). Breaking Bad: Existential Threat Decreases Pro-Environmental Behavior. *Basic & Applied Social Psychology, 39*(3), 153-166. doi:10.1080/01973533.2017.1296360

Carfora, Cavallo, Caso, Del Giudice, De Devitiis, Viscecchia, & Cicia. (2019). Explaining consumer purchase behavior for organic milk: Including trust and green self-identity within the theory of planned behavior. *Food Quality and Preference, 76*, 1-9. doi:10.1016/j.foodqual.2019.03.006

Carrigan, & Attalla. (2001). The myth of the ethical consumer – do ethics matter in purchase behaviour? *Journal of Consumer Marketing, 18*(7), 560-578. doi:10.1108/07363760110410263

Carrington, Neville, & Whitwell. (2010). Why Ethical Consumers Don't Walk Their Talk: Towards a Framework for Understanding the Gap Between the Ethical Purchase Intentions and Actual Buying Behaviour of Ethically Minded Consumers. *Journal of Business Ethics, 97*(1), 139-158. doi:10.1007/s10551-010-0501-6

Carrington, Neville, & Whitwell. (2014). Lost in translation: Exploring the ethical consumer intention–behavior gap. *Journal of Business Research, 67*(1), 2759-2767. doi:10.1016/j.jbusres.2012.09.022

Carrington, Zwick, & Neville. (2016). The ideology of the ethical consumption gap. *Marketing Theory, 16*(1), 21-38. doi:10.1177/1470593115595674

Caruana, Carrington, & Chatzidakis. (2016). Beyond the Attitude-Behaviour Gap: Novel Perspectives in Consumer Ethics': Introduction to the Thematic Symposium. *Journal of Business Ethics, 136*(2), 215-218. doi:10.1007/s10551-014-2444-9

Chai, Bradley, Lo, & Reser. (2015). What time to adapt? The role of discretionary time in sustaining the climate change value–action gap. *Ecological Economics, 116*, 95-107. doi:10.1016/j.ecolecon.2015.04.013

Chan. (2001). Determinants of Chinese consumers' green purchase behavior. *Psychology and Marketing, 18*(4), 389-413. doi:10.1002/mar.1013

Chatzidakis, Hibbert, & Smith. (2007). Why People Don't Take their Concerns about Fair Trade to the Supermarket: The Role of Neutralisation. *Journal of Business Ethics, 74*(1), 89-100. doi:10.1007/s10551-006-9222-2

Chatzidakis, Kastanakis, & Stathopoulou. (2016). Socio-Cognitive Determinants of Consumers' Support for the Fair Trade Movement. *Journal of Business Ethics, 133*(4), 95-109. doi:10.1007/s10551-014-2347-9

Cherrier, Szuba, & Özçağlar-Toulouse. (2012). Barriers to downward carbon emission: Exploring sustainable consumption in the face of the glass floor. *Journal of Marketing Management, 28*(3-4), 397-419. doi:10.1080/0267257x.2012.658835

Chung, & Monroe. (2003). Exploring Social Desirability Bias. *Journal of Business Ethics, 44*(4), 291-302. doi:10.1023/a:1023648703356

Cialdini. (2003). Crafting Normative Messages to Protect the Environment. *Current Directions in Psychological Science, 12*(4), 105-109. doi:10.1111/1467-8721.01242

Conner, Godin, Sheeran, & Germain. (2013). Some Feelings Are More Important: Cognitive Attitudes, Affective Attitudes, Anticipated Affect, and Blood Donation. *Health psychology: official journal of the Division of Health Psychology, American Psychological Association, 32*(3), 264–272. doi:10.1037/a0028500

Cooper-Martin, & Holbrook. (1993). Ethical Consumption Experiences and Ethical Space. *Advances in Consumer Research, 20*, 113-119.

Cowe, & Williams. (2000). *Who are the ethical consumers?* Retrieved from London: http://citeseerx.ist.psu.edu/viewdoc/download?doi=10.1.1.458.5207&rep=rep1&type=pdf

Crane, & Matten. (2004). *Business Ethics: A European Perspective : Managing Corporate Citizenship and Sustainability in the Age of Globalization*: Oxford University Press.

D'Astous, & Legendre. (2009). Understanding Consumers' Ethical Justifications: A Scale for Appraising Consumers' Reasons for Not Behaving Ethically. *Journal of Business Ethics, 87*(2), 255-268. doi:10.1007/s10551-008-9883-0

Davies, Foxall, & Pallister. (2002). Beyond the Intention–Behaviour Mythology: An Integrated Model of Recycling. *Marketing Theory, 2*(1), 29-113. doi:10.1177/1470593102002001645

Davies, Lee, & Ahonkhai. (2012). Do Consumers Care About Ethical-Luxury? *Journal of Business Ethics, 106*(1), 37-51. doi:10.1007/s10551-011-1071-y

De Groot, & Steg. (2009). Morality and Prosocial Behavior: The Role of Awareness, Responsibility, and Norms in the Norm Activation Model. *The Journal of Social Psychology, 149*(4), 425-449. doi:10.3200/socp.149.4.425-449

De Pelsmacker, & Janssens. (2007). A Model for Fair Trade Buying Behaviour: The Role of Perceived Quantity and Quality of Information and of Product-specific Attitudes. *Journal of Business Ethics, 75*(4), 361-380. doi:10.1007/s10551-006-9259-2

De Pelsmacker, Janssens, Sterckx, & Mielants. (2005). Consumer preferences for the marketing of ethically labelled coffee. *International Marketing Review, 22*(5), 512-530. doi:10.1108/02651330510624363

Dermody, Hanmer-Lloyd, Koenig-Lewis, & Zhao. (2015). Advancing sustainable consumption in the UK and China: the mediating effect of pro-environmental self-identity. *Journal of Marketing Management, 31*(13-14), 1472-1502. doi:10.1080/0267257X.2015.1061039

Di Giulio, Fischer, Schäfer, & Blättel-Mink. (2014). Conceptualizing sustainable consumption: toward an integrative framework. *Sustainability: Science, Practice and Policy, 10*(1), 45-61. doi:10.1080/15487733.2014.11908124

Diamantopoulos, Schlegelmilch, Sinkovics, & Bohlen. (2003). Can socio-demographics still play a role in profiling green consumers? A review of the evidence and an empirical investigation. *Journal of Business Research, 56*(6), 465-480. doi:https://doi.org/10.1016/S0148-2963(01)00241-7

Dolan. (2002). The Sustainability of "Sustainable Consumption". *Journal of Macromarketing, 22*(2), 170-181. doi:10.1177/0276146702238220

Doran. (2009). The Role of Personal Values in Fair Trade Consumption. *Journal of Business Ethics, 84*(4), 549-563. Retrieved from http://www.jstor.org/stable/40294760

Doran. (2010). Fair Trade Consumption: In Support of the Out-Group. *Journal of Business Ethics, 95*(4).

Eberhart, & Naderer. (2017). Quantitative and qualitative insights into consumers' sustainable purchasing behaviour: a segmentation approach based on motives and heuristic cues. *Journal of Marketing Management, 33*(13-14), 1149-1169. doi:10.1080/0267257x.2017.1371204

Eckhardt, Belk, & Devinney. (2010). Why don't consumers consume ethically? *Journal of Consumer Behaviour, 9*(6), 426-436. doi:10.1002/cb.332

Ehrich, & Irwin. (2005). Willful Ignorance in the Request for Product Attribute Information. *Journal of Marketing Research, 42*(3), 266-277. Retrieved from https://www.jstor.org/stable/30162371

Ellen, Wiener, & Cobb-Walgren. (1991). The Role of Perceived Consumer Effectiveness in Motivating Environmentally Conscious Behaviors. *Journal of Public Policy & Marketing, 10*(2), 102-117. Retrieved from http://www.jstor.org/stable/30000238

Englis, & Phillips. (2013). Does Innovativeness Drive Environmentally Conscious Consumer Behavior? *Psychology & Marketing, 30*(2), 160-172. doi:10.1002/mar.20595

Ertz, Karakas, & Sarigöllü. (2016). Exploring pro-environmental behaviors of consumers: An analysis of contextual factors, attitude, and behaviors. *Journal of Business Research, 69*(10), 3971-3980. doi:10.1016/j.jbusres.2016.06.010

European Commission. (2014). Directive 2014/95/EU of the European Parliament and of the council. *Official Journal of the European Union*.

Fischer, Michelsen, Birgit, & Di Giulio. (2012). Sustainable consumption: how to evaluate sustainability in consumption acts. In A. D. G. Rico Defila, Ruth Kaufmann-Hayoz (Ed.), *The Nature of Sustainable Consumption and How to Achieve it* (pp. 67-80): oekom.

Fisk. (1973). Criteria for a Theory of Responsible Consumption. *Journal of Marketing, 37*(2), 24-31. doi:10.2307/1250047

Gabler, Butler, & Adams. (2013). The environmental belief-behaviour gap: Exploring barriers to green consumerism. *Journal of Customer Behaviour, 12*(2/3), 159-176. doi:10.1362/147539213X13832198548292

Geiger, Fischer, & Schrader. (2017). Measuring What Matters in Sustainable Consumption: An Integrative Framework for the Selection of Relevant Behaviors. *Sustainable Development, 26*(1), 18-33. doi:10.1002/sd.1688

Gill, Crosby, & Taylor. (1986). Ecological Concern, Attitudes, and Social Norms in Voting Behavior. *The Public Opinion Quarterly, 50*(4), 537-554.

Gleim, Smith, Andrews, & Cronin. (2013). Against the Green: A Multi-method Examination of the Barriers to Green Consumption. *Journal of Retailing, 89*(1), 44-61. doi:10.1016/j.jretai.2012.10.001

Goldstein, Cialdini, & Griskevicius. (2008). A Room with a Viewpoint: Using Social Norms to Motivate Environmental Conservation in Hotels. *Journal of Consumer Research, 35*(3), 472-482. doi:10.1086/586910

Gollwitzer, & Sheeran. (2006). Implementation Intentions and Goal Achievement: A Meta-analysis of Effects and Processes. In *Advances in Experimental Social Psychology* (Vol. 38, pp. 69-119): Academic Press.

Govind, Singh, Garg, & D'Silva. (2019). Not Walking the Walk: How Dual Attitudes Influence Behavioral Outcomes in Ethical Consumption. *Journal of Business Ethics, 155*(4), 1195-1214. doi:10.1007/s10551-017-3545-z

Graafland. (2017). Religiosity, Attitude, and the Demand for Socially Responsible Products. *Journal of Business Ethics, 144*(1), 121-138. doi:10.1007/s10551-015-2796-9

Gregory-Smith, Smith, & Winklhofer. (2013). Emotions and dissonance in 'ethical' consumption choices. *Journal of Marketing Management, 29*(11-12), 1201-1223. doi:10.1080/0267257X.2013.796320

Grimmer, Kilburn, & Miles. (2016). The effect of purchase situation on realized pro-environmental consumer behavior. *Journal of Business Research, 69*(5), 1582-1586. doi:10.1016/j.jbusres.2015.10.021

Grob. (1995). A structural model of environmental attitudes and behaviour. *Journal of Environmental Psychology, 15*(3), 209-220. doi:10.1016/0272-4944(95)90004-7

Grønhøj, & Ölander. (2007). A gender perspective on environmentally related family consumption. *Journal of Consumer Behaviour, 6*(4), 218-235. doi:10.1002/cb.216

Grønhøj, & Thøgersen. (2012). Action speaks louder than words: The effect of personal attitudes and family norms on adolescents' pro-environmental behaviour. *Journal of Economic Psychology, 33*(1), 292-302. doi:10.1016/j.joep.2011.10.001

Gruber, & Schlegelmilch. (2014). How Techniques of Neutralization Legitimize Norm- and Attitude-Inconsistent Consumer Behavior. *Journal of Business Ethics, 121*(1), 29-45. doi:10.1007/s10551-013-1667-5

Guagnano, Stern, & Dietz. (1995). Influences on Attitude-Behavior Relationships. *Environment and Behavior, 27*(5), 699-718. doi:10.1177/0013916595275005

Gummerus, Liljander, & Sihlman. (2017). Do Ethical Social Media Communities Pay Off? An Exploratory Study of the Ability of Facebook Ethical Communities to Strengthen Consumers' Ethical Consumption Behavior. *Journal of Business Ethics, 144*(3), 449–465. doi:10.1007/s10551-015-2830-y

Gupta, & Agrawal. (2018). Environmentally Responsible Consumption: Construct Definition, Scale Development, and Validation. *Corporate Social Responsibility and Environmental Management, 25*(4), 523-536. doi:10.1002/csr.1476

Gupta, & Ogden. (2009). To buy or not to buy? A social dilemma perspective on green buying. *Journal of Consumer Marketing, 26*(6), 376-391. doi:10.1108/07363760910988201

Han, Seo, & Ko. (2017). Staging luxury experiences for understanding sustainable fashion consumption: A balance theory application. *Journal of Business Research, 74*, 162-167. doi:10.1016/j.jbusres.2016.10.029

Hanss, & Böhm. (2013). Promoting purchases of sustainable groceries: An intervention study. *Journal of Environmental Psychology, 33*, 53-67. doi:https://doi.org/10.1016/j.jenvp.2012.10.002

Harland, Staats, & Wilke. (2007). Situational and Personality Factors as Direct or Personal Norm Mediated Predictors of Pro-environmental Behavior: Questions Derived From Norm-activation Theory. *Basic & Applied Social Psychology, 29*(4), 323-334. doi:10.1080/01973530701665058

Hassan, Shiu, & Shaw. (2016). Who Says There is an Intention-Behaviour Gap? Assessing the Empirical Evidence of an Intention-Behaviour Gap in Ethical Consumption. *Journal of Business Ethics, 136*(2), 219-236. doi:10.1007/s10551-014-2440-0

Heath, O'Malley, Heath, & Story. (2016). Caring and Conflicted: Mothers' Ethical Judgments about Consumption. *Journal of Business Ethics, 136*(2), 237-250. doi:10.1007/s10551-014-2441-z

Hiller, & Woodall. (2019). Everything Flows: A Pragmatist Perspective of Trade-Offs and Value in Ethical Consumption. *Journal of Business Ethics, 157*(2). doi:10.1007/s10551-018-3956-5

Hines, Hungerford, & Tomera. (1987). Analysis and Synthesis of Research on Responsible Environmental Behavior: A Meta-Analysis. *The Journal of Environmental Education, 18*(2), 1-8. doi:10.1080/00958964.1987.9943482

Hira, & Ferrie. (2006). Fair Trade: Three Key Challenges for Reaching the Mainstream. *Journal of Business Ethics, 63*(2), 107-118. doi:10.1007/s10551-005-3041-8

Hoffmann, Mai, Lasarov, Krause, & Schmidt. (2019). Hungry bellies have no ears. How and why hunger inhibits sustainable consumption. *Ecological Economics, 160*(1), 96-104. doi:10.1016/j.ecolecon.2019.02.007

Homer, & Kahle. (1988). A Structural Equation Test of the Value-Attitude-Behavior Hierarchy. *Journal of Personality and Social Psychology, 54*(4), 638-646. doi:10.1037/0022-3514.54.4.638

Hunecke, Blöbaum, Matthies, & Hoeger. (2001). Responsibility and Environment Ecological Norm Orientation and External Factors in the Domain of Travel Mode Choice Behavior. *Environment and Behavior, 33*(1), 830-852. doi:10.1177/00139160121973269

Janssen. (2018). Determinants of organic food purchases: Evidence from household panel data. *Food Quality and Preference, 68*, 19-28. doi:https://doi.org/10.1016/j.foodqual.2018.02.002

Janssen, & Vanhamme. (2015). Theoretical Lenses for Understanding the CSR-Consumer Paradox. *Journal of Business Ethics, 130*(4), 775-787. doi:10.1007/s10551-014-2111-1

Jansson, Marell, & Nordlund. (2010). Green consumer behavior: determinants of curtailment and eco-innovation adoption. *Journal of Consumer Marketing, 27*(4), 358-370. doi:10.1108/07363761011052396

Johnstone, & Hooper. (2016). Social influence and green consumption behaviour: a need for greater government involvement. *Journal of Marketing Management, 32*(9-10), 827-855. doi:10.1080/0267257X.2016.1189955

Johnstone, & Lindh. (2018). The sustainability-age dilemma: A theory of (un)planned behaviour via influencers. *Journal of Consumer Behaviour, 17*(1), 127-139. doi:10.1002/cb.1693

Johnstone, & Tan. (2015). Exploring the Gap Between Consumers' Green Rhetoric and Purchasing Behaviour. *Journal of Business Ethics, 132*(2), 311-328. doi:10.1007/s10551-014-2316-3

Joshi, & Rahman. (2019). Consumers' Sustainable Purchase Behaviour: Modeling the Impact of Psychological Factors. *Ecological Economics, 159*, 235-243. doi:https://doi.org/10.1016/j.ecolecon.2019.01.025

Kadic-Maglajlic, Arslanagic-Kalajdzic, Micevski, Dlacic, & Zabkar. (2019). Being engaged is a good thing: Understanding sustainable consumption behavior among young adults. *Journal of Business Research, 104*. doi:10.1016/j.jbusres.2019.02.040

Kals, Schumacher, & Montada. (1999). Emotional Affinity toward Nature as a Motivational Basis to Protect Nature. *Environment and Behavior, 31*(2), 178-202. doi:10.1177/00139169921972056

Kilbourne, McDonagh, & Prothero. (1997). Sustainable Consumption and the Quality of Life: A Macromarketing Challenge to the Dominant Social Paradigm. *Journal of Macromarketing, 17*, 4-24. doi:10.1177/027614679701700103

Kilbourne, & Pickett. (2008). How materialism affects environmental beliefs, concern, and environmentally responsible behavior. *Journal of Business Research, 61*(9), 885-893. doi:10.1016/j.jbusres.2007.09.016

Kollmuss, & Agyeman. (2002). Mind the Gap: Why do people act environmentally and what are the barriers to pro-environmental behavior? *Environmental Education Research, 8*(3), 239-260. doi:10.1080/13504620220145401

Bibliography

Kronrod, Grinstein, & Wathieu. (2012). Go Green! Should Environmental Messages be So Assertive? *Journal of Marketing, 76*(1), 95-102. doi:10.1509/jm.10.0416

Kunchamboo, Lee, & Brace-Govan. (2017). Nature as extended-self: Sacred nature relationship and implications for responsible consumption behavior. *Journal of Business Research, 74*(1), 126-132. doi:10.1016/j.jbusres.2016.10.023

Kushwah, Dhir, & Sagar. (2019). Understanding consumer resistance to the consumption of organic food. A study of ethical consumption, purchasing, and choice behaviour. *Food Quality and Preference, 77*(1), 1-14. doi:10.1016/j.foodqual.2019.04.003

Lapiere. (1934). Attitudes vs. Actions. *Social Forces, 13*(2), 230-237. doi:10.2307/2570339

Leary, Vann, Mittelstaedt, Murphy, & Sherry. (2014). Changing the marketplace one behavior at a time: Perceived marketplace influence and sustainable consumption. *Journal of Business Research, 67*(9), 1953-1958. doi:10.1016/j.jbusres.2013.11.004

Leonidou, Leonidou, & Kvasova. (2010). Antecedents and outcomes of consumer environmentally friendly attitudes and behaviour. *Journal of Marketing Management, 26*(13-14), 1319-1344. doi:10.1080/0267257X.2010.523710

Lin, & Chang. (2012). Double Standard: The Role of Environmental Consciousness in Green Product Usage. *Journal of Marketing, 76*(5), 125-134. doi:10.1509/jm.11.0264

Lin, & Hsu. (2015). Using Social Cognitive Theory to Investigate Green Consumer Behavior. *24*(5), 326-343. doi:10.1002/bse.1820

Lin, & Huang. (2012). The influence factors on choice behavior regarding green products based on the theory of consumption values. *Journal of Cleaner Production, 22*(1), 11-18. doi:10.1016/j.jclepro.2011.10.002

Liu, Qu, Lei, & Jia. (2017). Understanding the Evolution of Sustainable Consumption Research. *Sustainable Development, 25*(5), 414-430. doi:10.1002/sd.1671

Longo, Shankar, & Nuttall. (2019). "It's Not Easy Living a Sustainable Lifestyle": How Greater Knowledge Leads to Dilemmas, Tensions and Paralysis. *Journal of Business Ethics, 154*(3), 759-779. doi:10.1007/s10551-016-3422-1

Lorenzoni, Nicholson-Cole, & Whitmarsh. (2007). Barriers perceived to engaging with climate change among the UK public and their policy implications. *Global Environmental Change, 17*(3), 445-459. doi:https://doi.org/10.1016/j.gloenvcha.2007.01.004

Luchs, Naylor, Irwin, & Raghunathan. (2010). The Sustainability Liability: Potential Negative Effects of Ethicality on Product Preference. *Journal of Marketing, 74*(5), 18-31. doi:10.1509/jmkg.74.5.18

Luchs, Phipps, & Hill. (2015). Exploring consumer responsibility for sustainable consumption. *Journal of Marketing Management, 31*(13-14), 1449-1471. doi:10.1080/0267257X.2015.1061584

Lundblad, & Davies. (2016). The values and motivations behind sustainable fashion consumption. *Journal of Consumer Behaviour, 15*(2), 149-162. doi:10.1002/cb.1559

Mai, Hoffmann, Lasarov, & Buhs. (2019). Ethical Products = Less Strong: How Explicit and Implicit Reliance on the Lay Theory Affects Consumption Behaviors. *Journal of Business Ethics, 158*(1). doi:10.1007/s10551-017-3669-1

Mainieri, Barnett, Valdero, Unipan, & Oskamp. (1997). Green Buying: The Influence of Environmental Concern on Consumer Behavior. *Journal of Social Psychology, 137*(2), 189-204. doi:10.1080/00224549709595430

Maxwell-Smith, Conway, Wright, & Olson. (2018). Translating Environmental Ideologies into Action: The Amplifying Role of Commitment to Beliefs. *Journal of Business Ethics, 153*(3), 839-858. doi:10.1007/s10551-016-3404-3

McCarty, & Shrum. (2001). The Influence of Individualism, Collectivism, and Locus of Control on Environmental Beliefs and Behavior. *Journal of Public Policy & Marketing, 20*(1), 93-104. doi:10.1509/jppm.20.1.93.17291

McDonald, Oates, Thyne, Alevizou, & McMorland. (2009). Comparing sustainable consumption patterns across product sectors. *International Journal of Consumer Studies, 33*(2), 137-145. doi:10.1111/j.1470-6431.2009.00755.x

McDonald, Oates, Thyne, Timmis, & Carlile. (2015). Flying in the face of environmental concern: why green consumers continue to fly. *Journal of Marketing Management, 31*(13-14), 1503-1528. doi:10.1080/0267257x.2015.1059352

Mittelstaedt, Shultz, Kilbourne, & Peterson. (2014). Sustainability as Megatrend. *Journal of Macromarketing, 34*(3), 253-264. doi:10.1177/0276146713520551

Mobley, Vagias, & Deward. (2010). Exploring Additional Determinants of Environmentally Responsible Behavior: The Influence of Environmental Literature and Environmental Attitudes. *Environment and Behavior, 42*(4), 420-447. doi:10.1177/0013916508325002

Moisander. (2007). Motivational complexity of green consumerism. *International Journal of Consumer Studies, 31*(4), 404-409. doi:10.1111/j.1470-6431.2007.00586.x

Moraes, Carrigan, Bosangit, Ferreira, & McGrath. (2017). Understanding Ethical Luxury Consumption Through Practice Theories: A Study of Fine Jewellery Purchases. *Journal of Business Ethics, 145*(3), 525-543. doi:10.1007/s10551-015-2893-9

Mostafa. (2007). A hierarchical analysis of the green consciousness of the Egyptian consumer. *Psychology and Marketing, 24*(5), 445-473. doi:10.1002/mar.20168

Mühlthaler, & Rademacher. (2017). The empowered consumer. *uwf UmweltWirtschaftsForum, 3-4*. doi:10.1007/s00550-017-0439-6

Nair, & Little. (2016). Context, Culture and Green Consumption: A New Framework. *Journal of International Consumer Marketing, 28*(3), 1-16. doi:10.1080/08961530.2016.1165025

Newholm, & Shaw. (2007). Studying the ethical consumer: a review of research. *Journal of Consumer Behaviour, 6*(5), 253-270. doi:10.1002/cb.225

Newhouse. (1990). Implications of Attitude and Behavior Research for Environmental Conservation. *The Journal of Environmental Education, 22*(1), 26-32. doi:10.1080/00958964.1990.9943043

Newman, Gorlin, & Dhar. (2014). When Going Green Backfires: How Firm Intentions Shape the Evaluation of Socially Beneficial Product Enhancements. *Journal of Consumer Research, 41*(3), 823-839.

Nicholls, & Lee. (2006). Purchase decision-making in fair trade and the ethical purchase 'gap': 'is there a fair trade twix?'. *Journal of Strategic Marketing, 14*(4), 369-386. doi:10.1080/09652540600956384

Norwegian Ministry of the Environment. (1994). Oslo roundtable on sustainable production and consumption. Retrieved from http://www.iisd.ca/consume/oslo004.html

Öberseder, Schlegelmilch, & Gruber. (2011). "Why Don't Consumers Care About CSR?": A Qualitative Study Exploring the Role of CSR in Consumption Decisions. *Journal of Business Ethics, 104*(4), 449-460. doi:10.1007/s10551-011-0925-7

Onwezen, Antonides, & Bartels. (2013). The Norm Activation Model: An exploration of the functions of anticipated pride and guilt in pro-environmental behaviour. *Journal of Economic Psychology, 39*(2), 141-153. doi:10.1016/j.joep.2013.07.005

Ozaki. (2011). Adopting sustainable innovation: what makes consumers sign up to green electricity? *Business Strategy & the Environment, 20*(1), 1-17. doi:10.1002/bse.650

Pagiaslis, & Krontalis. (2014). Green Consumption Behavior Antecedents: Environmental Concern, Knowledge, and Beliefs. *Psychology & Marketing, 31*(5), 335-348. doi:10.1002/mar.20698

Papaoikonomou, Ryan, & Ginieis. (2011). Towards a Holistic Approach of the Attitude Behaviour Gap in Ethical Consumer Behaviours: Empirical Evidence from Spain. *International Advances in Economic Research, 17*(1), 77-88. doi:10.1007/s11294-010-9288-6

Papista, Chrysochou, Krystallis, & Dimitriadis. (2018). Types of value and cost in consumer–green brands relationship and loyalty behaviour. *Journal of Consumer Behaviour, 17*(1), e101-e113. doi:10.1002/cb.1690

Park, & Lin. (2018). Exploring attitude–behavior gap in sustainable consumption: comparison of recycled and upcycled fashion products. *Journal of Business Research, in press.* doi:https://doi.org/10.1016/j.jbusres.2018.08.025

Peattie. (2010). Green Consumption: Behavior and Norms. *Annual Review of Environment and Resources, 35*(1), 195-228. doi:10.1146/annurev-environ-032609-094328

Pepper, Jackson, & Uzzell. (2009). An examination of the values that motivate socially conscious and frugal consumer behaviours. *International Journal of Consumer Studies, 33*(2), 126-136. doi:10.1111/j.1470-6431.2009.00753.x

Perera, Auger, & Klein. (2018). Green Consumption Practices Among Young Environmentalists: A Practice Theory Perspective. *Journal of Business Ethics, 152*(3), 843-864. doi:10.1007/s10551-016-3376-3

Petty, & Cacioppo. (1996). *Attitudes And Persuasion: Classic And Contemporary Approaches* New York: Westview Press.

Phipps, Ozanne, Luchs, Subrahmanyan, Kapitan, Catlin, . . . Weaver. (2013). Understanding the inherent complexity of sustainable consumption: A social cognitive framework. *Journal of Business Research, 66*(8), 1227-1234. doi:https://doi.org/10.1016/j.jbusres.2012.08.016

Poortinga, Steg, & Vlek. (2004). Values, Environmental Concern, and Environmental Behavior: A Study into Household Energy Use. *Environment and Behavior, 36*(1), 70-93. doi:10.1177/0013916503251466

Press, & Arnould. (2009). Constraints on Sustainable Energy Consumption: Market System and Public Policy Challenges and Opportunities. *Journal of Public Policy & Marketing, 28*(1), 102-113. doi:10.1509/jppm.28.1.102

Prothero, Dobscha, Freund, Kilbourne, Luchs, Ozanne, & Thøgersen. (2011). Sustainable Consumption: Opportunities for Consumer Research and Public Policy. *Journal of Public Policy & Marketing, 30*(1), 31-38. doi:10.1509/jppm.30.1.31

Rahman. (2018). The Interplay of Product Involvement and Sustainable Consumption: An Empirical Analysis of Behavioral Intentions Related to Green Hotels, Organic Wines and Green Cars. *Sustainable Development, 26*(4), 399-414. doi:10.1002/sd.1713

Rettie, Burchell, & Barnham. (2014). Social normalisation: Using marketing to make green normal. *Journal of Consumer Behaviour, 13*(1), 9-17. doi:10.1002/cb.1439

Rice. (2006). Pro-environmental Behavior in Egypt: Is there a Role for Islamic Environmental Ethics? *Journal of Business Ethics, 65*(4), 373-390. doi:10.1007/s10551-006-0010-9

Roberts. (1996a). Green consumers in the 1990s: Profile and implications for advertising. *Journal of Business Research, 36*(3), 217-231. doi:https://doi.org/10.1016/0148-2963(95)00150-6

Roberts. (1996b). Will the real socially responsible consumer please step forward? *Business Horizons, 39*(1), 79-83. doi:https://doi.org/10.1016/S0007-6813(96)90087-7

Roberts, & Bacon. (1997). Exploring the Subtle Relationships between Environmental Concern and Ecologically Conscious Consumer Behavior. *40*(1), 79-89. doi:10.1016/s0148-2963(96)00280-9

Romani, Grappi, & Bagozzi. (2016). Corporate Socially Responsible Initiatives and Their Effects on Consumption of Green Products. *Journal of Business Ethics, 135*(2), 253-264. doi:10.1007/s10551-014-2485-0

Rowlands, Scott, & Parker. (2003). Consumers and green electricity: profiling potential purchasers. *Business Strategy and the Environment, 12*(1), 36-48. doi:10.1002/bse.346

Rubik, Müller, Harnisch, Holzhauer, Schipperges, & Geiger. (2019). *Umweltbewusstsein in Deutschland 2018: Ergebnisse einer repräsentativen Bevölkerungsumfrage*. Retrieved from https://www.umweltbundesamt.de/publikationen/umweltbewusstsein-in-deutschland-2018

Russell, Young, Unsworth, & Robinson. (2017). Bringing habits and emotions into food waste behaviour. *Resources, Conservation and Recycling, 125*(1), 107-114. doi:10.1016/j.resconrec.2017.06.007

Sanne. (2002). Willing consumers—or locked-in? Policies for a sustainable consumption. *Ecological Economics, 42*(1), 273-287. doi:https://doi.org/10.1016/S0921-8009(02)00086-1

Schaefer, & Crane. (2005). Addressing Sustainability and Consumption. *Journal of Macromarketing, 25*(1), 76-92. doi:10.1177/0276146705274987

Schultz, Nolan, Cialdini, Goldstein, & Griskevicius. (2007). The Constructive, Destructive, and Reconstructive Power of Social Norms. *Psychological Science, 18*(5), 429-434. doi:10.1111/j.1467-9280.2007.01917.x

Schwartz. (1977). Normative Influences on Altruism. In L. Berkowitz (Ed.), *Advances in Experimental Social Psychology* (Vol. 10, pp. 221-279): Academic Press.

Schwarz. (2007). Attitude construction: Evaluation in context. *Social Cognition, 25*(5), 638-656. doi:10.1521/soco.2007.25.5.638

Scott, & Weaver. (2018). The Intersection of Sustainable Consumption and Anticonsumption: Repurposing to Extend Product Life Spans. *Journal of Public Policy & Marketing, 37*(2), 291-305. doi:10.1177/0743915618811851

Shang, & Peloza. (2015). Can "Real" Men Consume Ethically? How Ethical Consumption Leads to Unintended Observer Inference. *Journal of Business Ethics, 139*(1). doi:10.1007/s10551-015-2627-z

Shaw, & Clarke. (1999). Belief formation in ethical consumer groups: an exploratory study. *Marketing Intelligence & Planning, 17*(2), 109-120. doi:10.1108/02634509910260968

Shaw, Grehan, Shiu, Hassan, & Thomson. (2005). An exploration of values in ethical consumer decision making. *Journal of Consumer Behaviour, 4*(3), 185-200. doi:10.1002/cb.3

Shaw, & Shiu. (2002). An assessment of ethical obligation and self-identity in ethical consumer decision-making: a structural equation modelling approach. *International Journal of Consumer Studies, 26*(4), 286-293. doi:10.1046/j.1470-6431.2002.00255.x

Shaw, & Shiu. (2003). Ethics in consumer choice: a multivariate modelling approach. *European Journal of Marketing, 37*(10), 1485-1498. doi:10.1108/03090560310487202

Shaw, Shiu, Hassan, Bekin, & Hogg. (2007). Intending To Be Ethical: An Examination of Consumer Choice in Sweatshop Avoidance. *Advances in Consumer Research, 34*(1).

Sheeran. (2002). Intention—Behavior Relations: A Conceptual and Empirical Review. *European Review of Social Psychology, 12*(1), 1-36. doi:10.1080/14792772143000003

Song, & Kim. (2018). Theory of Virtue Ethics: Do Consumers' Good Traits Predict Their Socially Responsible Consumption? *Journal of Business Ethics, 152*(4), 1159-1175. doi:10.1007/s10551-016-3331-3

Spence, Poortinga, & Pidgeon. (2012). The Psychological Distance of Climate Change. *Risk Analysis, 32*(6), 957-972. doi:10.1111/j.1539-6924.2011.01695.x

Steg, & Vlek. (2009). Encouraging pro-environmental behaviour: An integrative review and research agenda. *Journal of Environmental Psychology, 29*(3), 309-317. doi:10.1016/j.jenvp.2008.10.004

Stern, & Dietz. (1994). The Value Basis of Environmental Concern. *Journal of Social Issues, 50*(3), 65-84. doi:10.1111/j.1540-4560.1994.tb02420.x

Straughan. (1999). Environmental segmentation alternatives: a look at green consumer behavior in the new millennium. *Journal of Consumer Marketing, 16*(6), 558-575. doi:10.1108/07363769910297506

Strubel. (2017). *Nachhaltiger Konsum, Fairer Handel und Gerechtigkeit: Eine multimethodale psychologische Untersuchung gerechtigkeits- und verantwortungsbezogener Motive.* (PhD). Katholische Universität Eichstätt-Ingolstadt, Frankfurt am Main.

Sutton. (1998). Predicting and Explaining Intentions and Behavior: How Well Are We Doing? *Journal of Applied Social Psychology, 28*(15), 1317-1338. doi:10.1111/j.1559-1816.1998.tb01679.x

Szmigin, Carrigan, & McEachern. (2009). The conscious consumer: taking a flexible approach to ethical behaviour. *International Journal of Consumer Studies, 33*(2), 224-231. doi:10.1111/j.1470-6431.2009.00750.x

Tan, Johnstone, & Yang. (2016). Barriers to green consumption behaviours: The roles of consumers' green perceptions. *Australasian Marketing Journal (AMJ), 24*(4), 288-299. doi:10.1016/j.ausmj.2016.08.001

Tanner, & Wölfing Kast. (2003). Promoting Sustainable Consumption: Determinants of Green Purchases by Swiss Consumers. *Psychology & Marketing, 20*(10), 883-902. doi:10.1002/mar.10101

Tarkiainen, & Sundqvist. (2009). Product involvement in organic food consumption: Does ideology meet practice? *Psychology & Marketing, 26*(9), 844-863. doi:10.1002/mar.20302

Thøgersen. (1994). A model of recycling behaviour, with evidence from Danish source separation programmes. *International Journal of Research in Marketing, 11*(2), 145-163. doi:10.1016/0167-8116(94)90025-6

Thøgersen. (2005). How May Consumer Policy Empower Consumers for Sustainable Lifestyles? *Journal of Consumer Policy, 28*(2), 143-177. doi:10.1007/s10603-005-2982-8

Thøgersen, & Olander. (2002). Human Values and the Emergence of a Sustainable Consumption Pattern: A Panel Study. *Journal of Economic Psychology, 23*(4), 605-630. doi:10.1016/S0167-4870(02)00120-4

Thøgersen, & Ölander. (2003). Spillover of environment-friendly consumer behaviour. *Journal of Environmental Psychology, 23*(3), 225-236. doi:https://doi.org/10.1016/S0272-4944(03)00018-5

Thøgersen, & Zhou. (2012). Chinese consumers' adoption of a 'green' innovation – The case of organic food. *Journal of Marketing Management, 28*(3-4), 313-333. doi:10.1080/0267257X.2012.658834

Tilikidou, & Delistavrou. (2008). Types and influential factors of consumers' non-purchasing ecological behaviors. *Business Strategy & the Environment (John Wiley & Sons, Inc), 17*(1), 61-76. doi:10.1002/bse.500

Torma, Aschemann-Witzel, & Thøgersen. (2018). I nudge myself: Exploring 'self-nudging' strategies to drive sustainable consumption behaviour. *International Journal of Consumer Studies, 42*(1), 141-154. doi:10.1111/ijcs.12404

Triandis. (1977). *Interpersonal behavior*. Monterey, CA: Books/Cole.

Triandis. (1980). Values, attitudes, and interpersonal behavior. In H. H. M. Page (Ed.), *Nebraska symposium on motivation* (Vol. 27, pp. 195-259). Lincoln, Neb.: University of Nebraska Press.

Trudel. (2018). Sustainable consumer behavior. *Consumer Psychology Review, 2*(1). doi:10.1002/arcp.1045

United Nations. (1992). *Agenda 21*. Paper presented at the United Nations Conference on Environment & Development, Rio de Janerio, Brazil. https://sustainabledevelopment.un.org/content/documents/Agenda21.pdf

United Nations. (2019). Sustainable Development Goals. Retrieved from https://sustainabledevelopment.un.org/?menu=1300

Urien, & Kilbourne. (2011). Generativity and self-enhancement values in eco-friendly behavioral intentions and environmentally responsible consumption behavior. *Psychology & Marketing, 28*(1), 69-90. doi:10.1002/mar.20381

Vainio, & Paloniemi. (2014). The complex role of attitudes toward science in pro-environmental consumption in the Nordic countries. *Ecological Economics, 108*(3), 18-27. doi:10.1016/j.ecolecon.2014.09.026

Valor, & Carrero. (2014). Viewing Responsible Consumption as a Personal Project. *Psychology & Marketing, 31*(12), 1110-1121. doi:10.1002/mar.20758

van Dam. (2016). *Sustainable Consumption And Marketing.* (PhD PhD thesis). Wageningen University, Wageningen, The Netherlands.

Vassallo, Scalvedi, & Saba. (2016). Investigating psychosocial determinants in influencing sustainable food consumption in Italy. *International Journal of Consumer Studies, 40*(4), 422-434. doi:10.1111/ijcs.12268

Vermeir, & Verbeke. (2006). Sustainable Food Consumption: Exploring the Consumer "Attitude – Behavioral Intention" Gap. *Journal of Agricultural and Environmental Ethics, 19*(2), 169-194. doi:10.1007/s10806-005-5485-3

Vermeir, & Verbeke. (2008). Sustainable food consumption among young adults in Belgium: Theory of planned behaviour and the role of confidence and values. *Ecological Economics, 64*(3), 542-553. doi:https://doi.org/10.1016/j.ecolecon.2007.03.007

Verplanken, Aarts, Knippenberg, & Knippenberg. (1994). Attitude Versus General Habit: Antecedents of Travel Mode Choice. *Journal of Applied Social Psychology, 24*(4), 285-300. doi:10.1111/j.1559-1816.1994.tb00583.x

Verplanken, & Wood. (2006). Interventions to Break and Create Consumer Habits. *Journal of Public Policy & Marketing, 25*(1), 90-103. doi:10.1509/jppm.25.1.90

Viscusi, Huber, & Bell. (2011). Promoting Recycling: Private Values, Social Norms, and Economic Incentives. *American Economic Review, 101*(3), 65-70. doi:10.1257/aer.101.3.65

Vlaeminck, Jiang, & Vranken. (2014). Food labeling and eco-friendly consumption: Experimental evidence from a Belgian supermarket. *Ecological Economics, 108*(3), 180-190. doi:10.1016/j.ecolecon.2014.10.019

Wang, Lin, & Li. (2018). Exploring the effects of non-cognitive and emotional factors on household electricity saving behavior. *Energy Policy, 115*, 171-180. doi:10.1016/j.enpol.2018.01.012

Webb, Mohr, & Harris. (2008). A re-examination of socially responsible consumption and its measurement. *Journal of Business Research, 61*, 91-98. doi:10.1016/j.jbusres.2007.05.007

Webster. (1975). Determining the Characteristics of the Socially Conscious Consumer. *Journal of Consumer Research, 2*(3), 188-196. doi:10.1086/208631

Welsch, & Kühling. (2009). Determinants of pro-environmental consumption: The role of reference groups and routine behavior. *Ecological Economics, 69*(1), 166-176. doi:https://doi.org/10.1016/j.ecolecon.2009.08.009

White, & Simpson. (2013). When Do (and Don't) Normative Appeals Influence Sustainable Consumer Behaviors? *Journal of Marketing, 77*(2), 78-95. doi:10.1509/jm.11.0278

Wiederhold, & Martinez. (2018). Ethical consumer behaviour in Germany: The attitude-behaviour gap in the green apparel industry. *International Journal of Consumer Studies, 42*(4), 419-429. doi:10.1111/ijcs.12435

Wilson, Lindsey, & Schooler. (2000). A model of dual attitudes. *Psychological Review, 107*(1), 101-126. doi:10.1037/0033-295X.107.1.101

Yang, & Weber. (2019). Who can improve the environment—Me or the powerful others? An integrative approach to locus of control and pro-environmental behavior in China. *Resources, Conservation and Recycling, 146*(2), 55-67. doi:10.1016/j.resconrec.2019.03.005

Yeow, Dean, & Tucker. (2014). Bags for Life: The Embedding of Ethical Consumerism. *Journal of Business Ethics, 125*(1), 87-99. doi:10.1007/s10551-013-1900-2

Young, Hwang, McDonald, & Oates. (2010). Sustainable consumption: green consumer behaviour when purchasing products. *Sustainable Development, 18*(1), 20-31. doi:10.1002/sd.394

Young, Russell, Robinson, & Chintakayala. (2018). Sustainable Retailing – Influencing Consumer Behaviour on Food Waste. *Business Strategy & the Environment (John Wiley & Sons, Inc), 27*(1), 1-15. doi:10.1002/bse.1966

Zane, Irwin, & Walker Reczek. (2015). Do less ethical consumers denigrate more ethical consumers? The effect of willful ignorance on judgments of others. *Journal of Consumer Psychology, 26*(3), 337-349. doi:10.1016/j.jcps.2015.10.002

Zaval, Markowitz, & Weber. (2015). How Will I Be Remembered? Conserving the Environment for the Sake of One's Legacy. *Psychological Science, 26*(2), 231-236. doi:10.1177/0956797614561266

Appendix

Appendix A: Definitions of sustainable consumption and related constructs

Author & Year	Definition	Key elements
Own definition	**Sustainable consumption** is the selection, acquisition, use and disposal of products and services that considers not only the consumer's own needs and wants, but also the ones of the current and future population in both an ecological and social respect.	(a) entire consumption cycle, (b) ecological and social issues, (c) global population and (d) long-term perspective
Geiger et al. (2017)	"**Sustainable consumption behaviors** [are] individual acts of satisfying needs in different areas of life by acquiring, using and disposing goods and services that do not compromise the ecological and socio-economic conditions of all people (currently living or in the future) to satisfy their own needs." (p.20)	(a), (b), (c), (d) and highlights that consumption serves the satisfaction of one's needs
Di Giulio et al. (2014)	"[T]he **sustainability of consumption acts** is defined by the degree to which individual acts of selecting, acquiring, using, and disposing of, or prosuming goods contribute to creating or sustaining external conditions that allow all human beings to meet their objective needs today and in the future. These external conditions comprise ecological, social, cultural, and economic resources and processes." (p.54)	(a), (b), (c), (d) and explicitly mentions the cultural and economic component of sustainable consumption
Phipps et al. (2013)	"**Sustainable consumption** [is] consumption that simultaneously optimizes the environmental, social, and economic consequences of acquisition, use and disposition in order to meet the needs of both current and future generations" (p.1227)	(a), (b), (c) and (d)
Pepper et al. (2009)	"**Sustainable consumption** is a broad and contested concept that concerns the interaction of social and ecological issues such as environmental protection, human needs, quality of life, and intra-generational and inter-generational equity." (p.126)	(b), (c), (d) and stresses the width of as well as the controversial nature of this concept
Vermeir and Verbeke (2006)	"**Sustainable consumption** is based on a decision-making process that takes the consumer's social responsibility into account in addition to individual needs and wants." (p.170)	(b) and empathizes that consumption serves to satisfy both needs *and* wants

Author & Year	Definition	Key elements
Kilbourne et al. (1997)	**Sustainable consumption** "minimizes environmental effects, considers the needs of future generations, and is for the satisfaction of needs that produce a better quality of life". (p. 5)	(c), (d) and highlights that consumption serves the satisfaction of one's needs
Norwegian Ministry of the Environment (1994)	**Sustainable production and consumption** is "[t]he use of goods and related products which respond to basic needs and bring a better quality of life, while minimizing the use of natural resources and toxic materials as well as the emissions of waste and pollutants over the life cycle, so as not to jeopardize the needs of future generations."	(c) and (d)
Concepts related to sustainable consumption		
Kushwah et al. (2019)	"[..] **ethical consumption** [is] an act of buying products that consider various ethical attributes (e.g., human, environment, animal, etc.) besides the essential product benefits based on individual moral beliefs and values. (p.3)	(b) and shows that ethical consumption is based on a person's moral beliefs and values but
Crane and Matten (2004)	"**Ethical consumption** is the conscious and deliberate choice to make certain consumption choices due to personal and moral beliefs." (p.15)	Also shows that ethical consumption is based on a person's moral beliefs and values but
Tan, Johnstone, and Yang (2016)	"Several definitions were found in the literature [..]. Commonly, consumers' **green consumption behaviour** includes recycling, protecting waterways, bringing own shopping bags, the purchase and consumption of environmentally-friendly products etc." (p.289)	Shows that green consumption has no clear and consistent definition and may include social as well as ecological issues (b)
Balderjahn et al. (2013)	"**Consciousness for sustainable consumption** (CSC) [is] an intention to consume in a way that enhances the environmental, social and economic aspects of quality of life." (p.182)	(b) and explicitly mentions the economic component of sustainable consumption
Steg and Vlek (2009)	**Pro-environmental behavior** refers to "behavior that harms the environment as little as possible, or even benefits the environment" (p.309)	Consideration of the ecological component only
Fisk (1973)	"**Responsible consumption** refers to rational and efficient use of resources with respect to the global human population" (p. 24)	(c) and stresses the underlying resources used for consuming

Appendix B: Overview of justification strategies found in the literature

Authors	Exemplary argumentation	Key theme
Chatzidakis et al. (2007), and Gruber et al. (2014)	"It so much more expensive anyway, and to be honest money is so tight at the moment…" or "I think I would become more passionate about FT (Fair Trade) products if I had realized the difference that exists when a product is FT and when it's not…but, I think people don't know enough, they are not given much explanation…" (Chatzidakis et al., 2007, p.92) "I don't think I would consider sustainability when shopping. It's not OK what most companies do, but I haven't asked them to do it. Whether I care or not they would do it anyway." (Gruber et al., 2014, p.40)	Denial of responsibility (asserting that consumers should not be held accountable for sustainability issues)
Chatzidakis et al. (2007) and Gruber et al. (2014)	"I wouldn't feel bad for not buying FT…in my view, the causes of unfair trade are systemic… (by buying FT) I'm not doing anything that contributes to an improved trading system." or "I think, the problem is too big to be dealt at the level of the consumer… it seems to me that the minority of people that care about FT aren't going to overcome the bigger problem…which is about all those organizations and subsidies, signing agreements". (Chatzidakis et al., 2007, p.92) "It's much better for children to work for a minimum wage than to do nothing and die. Presumably, they are happy about every cent they earn. Actually you are just helping them, doing good by buying their products." (Gruber et al., 2014, p.40)	Denial of injury or of benefit (claiming that they harmed nobody or their behavior would not benefit anyone)
Chatzidakis et al. (2007) and Gruber et al. (2014)	"I think that the issue of FT puts a lot of burden of fairness to the consumer… for example, you've got COSTA coffee, where if you look at the menu, it says in small print letters that you can request any of our coffees in FT…where maybe it should be the other way round? If a person wants to save some money they could request non-FT coffee" (Chatzidakis et al., 2007, p.92) This also contains denial of responsibility. "Even if a company really behaves irresponsibly, it's pointless to be the only person not going there. Then I pay a lot more somewhere else and other people continue to shop for cheap things. Then it doesn't make a difference." (Gruber et al., 2014, p.40)	Condemning the condemners (putting the blame on the companies)

Appendix

Authors	Exemplary argumentation	Key theme
Chatzidakis et al. (2007), and Gruber et al. (2014)	"...to be honest, I like trying different things...and I am not very keen on buying the same on and on". "FT might be a consideration, but in general...when I go shopping in Sainsbury's I look for the cheapest and nearest thing to me" (Chatzidakis et al., 2007, p.92) "She doesn't have enough money but still wants to cater for everything her children want. Also she doesn't want the children to notice that they cannot have a lot. She buys cheaper stuff so her children have something and will not be ragged at school" (Gruber et al., 2014, p.40)	Appeal to higher loyalties (referring to domestic circumstanced that have an impact on the consumer's decision making)
Gruber et al. (2014)	"Concerning boycotting Nestle' [...] nowadays it's not possible to do that anymore, I wouldn't do this because so many products have a name that doesn't reveal the company behind it, it's not possible" (Gruber et al., 2014, p.40)	Defense of the necessity (consumers claiming that they lack the possibility to engage in the desired behavior)
Gruber et al. (2014)	"I assume that the average consumer, in such a situation, would list random examples of how he or she has already contributed to saving the environment. They say that they have already done something, so they don't have to pay in this specific situation." (Gruber et al., 2014, p.40)	Claim of the metaphor of the ledger (consumers thinking that they have already made their contribution)
Gruber et al. (2014)	"I think if a company offers a good product that is extremely cheap then consumers would buy it anyway, even if the company is engaging in dubious practices and not working in a sustainable way. It is just the best product and I think the personal advantage is of greater importance (...) One's own benefit is greater and more important than the benefit you see if workers in Asia are doing better." (Gruber et al., 2014, p.41)	Claim of entitlement (consumers thinking they deserve the extra benefit a specific purchase brings about)
Gruber et al. (2014)	"I wouldn't get a bad conscience if I did it like this. Knowing that others who, in my eyes, should really have a bad conscience are just doing whatever they feel like." (Gruber et al., 2014, p.41)	Claim of relative acceptability (referring to others that are even worse in their behavior)
Gruber et al. (2014)	"I am a more important person and I don't care about other people, that is why I don't really mind this product being made by a poorer person and I am interested in my own advantage." (Gruber et al., 2014, p.41)	Claim of individuality (consumer is occupied with his/herself)
Gruber et al. (2014)	"The product in front of me is exactly as bad as the others. It is attached to the same	Justification by comparison

Appendix

Authors	Exemplary argumentation	Key theme
	unethical production. And if I stand in front of the shelf and there are five products and all five products are equally bad I can only choose the lesser of two evils" (Gruber et al., 2014, p.41)	(referring to even worse conducts (not to behavior of others))
The following neutralization techniques were found in relation to ethical consumer behavior and thus also rarely contain behaviors that are not related to sustainability (e.g. copyright infringement)		
Eckhardt et al. (2010)	"I might consider a local brand not using bad labor practices, but it would have to be competitive in terms of all other factors." (Eckhardt et al., 2010, p.430)	Economic rationalization (focusing on personal utility)
Eckhardt et al. (2010)	'Now we're part of Europe, so it's Europe's responsibility." "I cannot do anything about it, so why bother thinking about it." (Eckhardt et al., 2010, p.431)	Institutional dependency (similar to denial of responsibility, as responsibility is ascribed to institutions)
Eckhardt et al. (2010)	"What can we do? It has nothing to do with us. Some people earn well, some countries are poor. That is business. It's cheap for them [Nike]. If they try to do it in the US, they have to pay more. There is nothing wrong. If they [the workers] had no job, then how would it be? At least they have food to eat." (Eckhardt et al., 2010, p.430)	Developmental realism (economic growth works like this)
The following rationalizations are related to flying by plane		
McDonald et al. (2015)	"People fly internally in this country, I don't, but say you needed to get from London to Scotland, getting the train would be so horrendous, and it's just hideous and expensive and takes so long." (McDonald et al., 2015, p.1512)	Justifications related to travel product (e.g. more convenient or less expensive)
McDonald et al. (2015)	"I have flown three times over four years to do international work on sustainability with the [developing nation] government, which I think is justified." (McDonald et al., 2015, p.1513)	Justifications related to travel context (e.g. for work of visiting friends)
McDonald et al. (2015)	"There's this breadth of experience that comes from travelling, that you've seen this and you've done that, sometimes I feel like I'm under pressure to travel because that's what all the interesting people have done...I think that other people judge us by our travelling experiences." (McDonald et al., 2015, p.1513)	Justifications related to personal identity (i.e. benefits for oneself)

Appendix C: Graphical representation of the research methods that were used in the reviewed articles

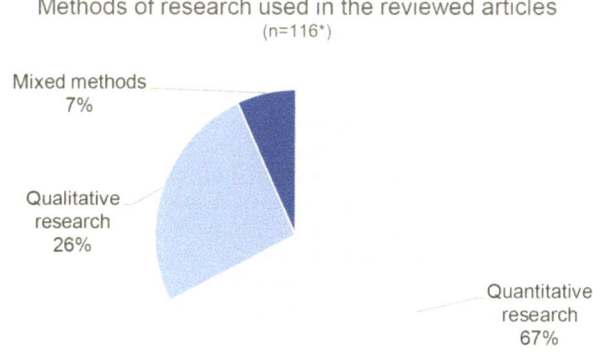

*The sample size is only 116 because two of the papers did not explicitly undertake research for the article cited in this thesis, which is why they were excluded here.

Appendix D: Graphical representation of the proportion of the reviewed articles that either studied purchasing behavior only or different behaviors at once

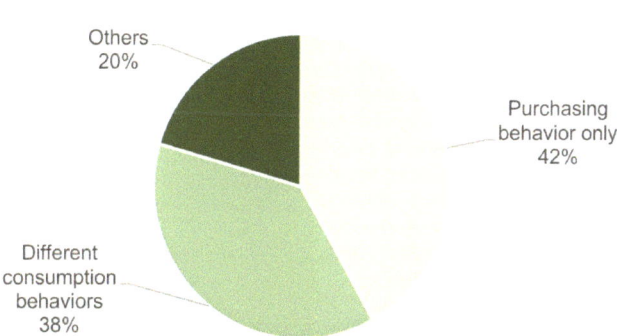

*The sample size is only 116 because two of the papers were meta-analysis and therefore automatically research different behaviors, which is why they were excluded here.

Appendix E: Graphical representation of the industries that are studied in the articles that focused on a specific behavior

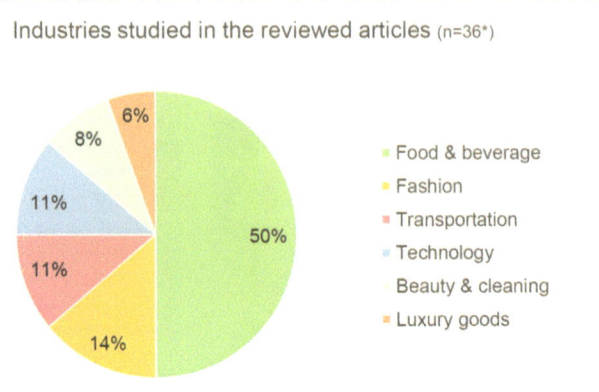

*The industry is only displayed in the graph if there was a specific behavior studied, only one industry was examined and this industry appeared more than once in the literature reviewed.